BASKETBALL

LEGENDS

BASKETBALL
LEGENDS

GREG GARBER

© George Long/Sports Illustrated

FRIEDMAN/FAIRFAX PUBLISHERS

A FRIEDMAN/FAIRFAX BOOK

Copyright © 1993 by Michael Friedman Publishing Group, Inc.

ISBN 1-56799-030-4

Editor: Bruce J. Lubin
Designer: David Shultz
Art Director: Jeff Batzli
Photography Editor: Christopher C. Bain

Typeset by BPE Graphics, Inc.
Color separations by South Sea International Press, Ltd.
Printed and bound in Hong Kong by Leefung-Asco Printers Ltd.

For bulk purchases and special sales, please contact:
Friedman/Fairfax Publishers
15 West 26 Street
New York, NY 10010
(212) 685-6610   FAX (212) 685-1307

D E D I C A T I O N For John Daniel Flynn, whose technological pyrotechnics continue to amaze me.

ACKNOWLEDGMENTS To my father, for bolting the backboard and rim to the barn so that two brothers could test each other; special thanks to Wayne R. Patterson, research specialist at the Basketball Hall of Fame; Peter May of the *Hartford Courant*; Garry Brown, the fine writer at the *Springfield Union* and *Republican*; the statistical hounds at the Elias Sports Bureau; Bruce Lubin, vice president and editor at Michael Friedman Publishing Group, Inc.

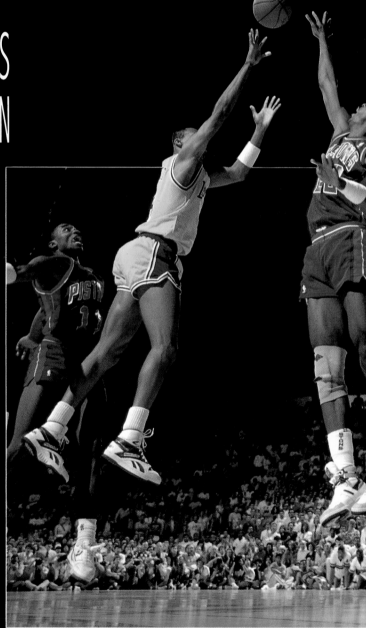

TABLE OF
CONTENTS

9 INTRODUCTION

The Los Angeles Lakers won their fifth NBA title of the 1980s by downing the Detroit Pistons, 108-105, in game seven of the championship series on June 21, 1988.

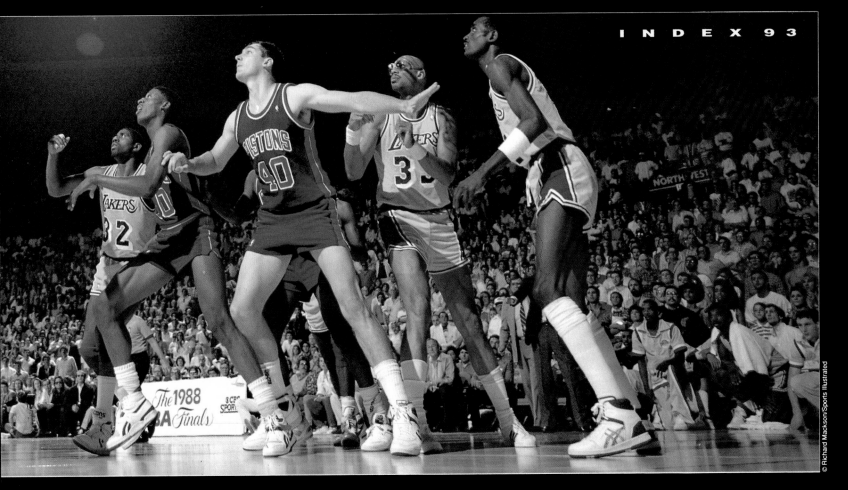

THE
10 LEGENDS

THE GREATEST
60 GAMES

THE GREATEST
76 MOMENTS

INDEX 93

INTRODUCTION

O ver the course of history, the legends of basketball have come in all shapes and guises. Manute Bol, the 7-foot-6 Dinka tribesman, is not exactly an offensive force in the National Basketball Association. At 225 pounds, he resembles a healthy sapling with the appropriate vertical leap and lateral movement. Still, there is a place in the NBA for Bol because he is a natural shot blocker. In 1985–86, Bol snuffed 397 shots—good for the league's best total. That same season, a 5-foot-7 guard named Anthony Jerome Webb first made the Atlanta Hawks roster. He grew up in Dallas, Texas, where they called him "Spud." When the Hawks' regulars started to sag late in the first quarter, Webb, bouncing like a water-bug, came in to create instant offense and more than a little havoc. Bol and Webb, of course, represent the long and the short of the players in today's professional game.

Kareem Abdul-Jabbar, the greatest scorer in the history of the game, stood a resounding 7-foot-2, weighed 267 pounds, and even at the age of 41 maintained the reflexes of a cat. Red Auerbach, at 5-foot-10 and 170 pounds, averaged all of six points over his college career, but grew to become the greatest coach the sport has ever known,

winning 938 games in 20 seasons and nine straight championships.

Michael Jordan, the high-flying guard for the Chicago Bulls, has a chance to finish his career with the best scoring average ever. At a mere 6-foot-6, 195 pounds, he is small by NBA standards, but he moves among the wide-bodies with unmatched athleticism. Larry Bird of the Boston Celtics, the league's Most Valuable Player for three consecutive years, took a more deliberate, even plodding, approach, yet his instinct for the game was, at times, a little frightening.

Wilt Chamberlain and Bill Russell, who played opposite each other at center for a decade, may have enjoyed the greatest individual rivalry in professional sports. Chamberlain, at 7-foot-1, was probably the most dominant offensive player ever, while the 6-foot-10 Russell claims the defensive title. Pete Maravich, who grew up in the Carolinas, and Lynette Woodard, a native of Kansas, both shared dreams of success in basketball. Today they are the first- and second-highest career scorers in college history.

Here are the greats of the game, from Abdul-Jabbar to John Wooden, his coach at UCLA.

THE LEGENDS

The legends of basketball have come in all shapes and sizes over time. Manute Bol, the 7-foot-6 Dinka tribesman, is not exactly an offensive force in the NBA. At 225 pounds, he resembles a healthy sapling with the appropriate vertical leap and lateral movement. Still, there is a place in the NBA for Bol because he is a natural shot blocker. In the 1985–86 season, Bol snuffed 397 shots—good for the league's best total. That same season, a 5-foot-7 guard named Anthony Jerome Webb made the Atlanta Hawks roster. He grew up in Dallas, Texas, where they called him Spud. When the Hawks' regulars started to sag late in the first quarter, Webb bouncing like a water-

bug, came in to create instant offense and more than a little havoc. Bol and Webb, of course, represent the long and the short of the players in today's professional game.

Kareem Abdul-Jabbar, the greatest scorer in the history of the game, is a resounding 7-foot-2, 267 pounds, and, even in his forties, maintains the reflexes of a cat. Red Auerbach, 5-foot-10, 170 pounds, averaged all of 6 points per game during his college career, but grew to become the greatest coach the sport has ever known,

winning 938 games in twenty seasons and nine straight championships.

Michael Jordan, the high-flying guard for the Chicago Bulls, has a chance to finish his career with the best scoring average ever. At a mere 6-foot-6, 195 pounds, small by NBA standards, Jordan moves among the widebodies with unmatched athletic ability. Larry Bird of the Boston Celtics, winner of the league's Most Valuable Player award for three consecutive years, has more of a deliberate, plodding ap-

proach. Yet Bird's instinct for the game is, at times, uncanny and amazing.

Wilt Chamberlain and Bill Russell, who played opposite each other at center for a decade, may have enjoyed the greatest individual rivalry in professional sport. Chamberlain, at 7-foot-1, was probably the most dominant offensive player ever; the 6-foot-10 Russell claims the defensive title. Both Pete Maravich and Lynette Woodard shared dreams of success in basketball; today they are the highest and second-highest career scorers, respectively, in college history.

Compiled here are the greats of the game, from Abdul-Jabbar to John Wooden, his coach at UCLA.

The Boston Celtics' Rick Robey (opposite page) approaches seven-feet tall, but he is helpless against Kareem Abdul-Jabbar's unstoppable Skyhook.

KAREEM
ABDUL-JABBAR

© Mike Valeri/FPG International

Kareem Abdul-Jabbar was always the first player listed in the National Basketball Association Register and, coincidentally, the all-time leader in games played and points scored. He is unique in another way. Over the years, the 7-foot-2 center developed something generations of players have vainly sought: an unblockable shot. It is called the Skyhook, and when Abdul-Jabbar has it working, it is the ultimate weapon. No one can touch it.

When he retired after the 1988–89 season, Jabbar had scored 38,387 points, and many of them immediately followed the familiar Skyhook, in which Abdul-Jabbar dribbled baseline, his back to the basket, pivoted, planted his left foot and spread out his left elbow, leapt, and flipped the ball toward the basket with his massive right arm in a soft, short, arc. Because of his height and jumping ability, Abdul-Jabbar's Skyhook was actually released above the basket. Gravity, the goaltending rule, and years of practice made it impossible to defend against. After he loosed a Skyhook on April 5, 1984, against the Utah Jazz, Abdul-Jabbar passed Wilt Chamberlain as the league's career scoring leader.

The amazing numbers seen in his NBA resume—as the most-decorated player ever, Abdul-Jabbar also leads all players in field goals attempted (28,307) and made (15,837), blocked shots (3,189), and personal fouls (4,657)—can be traced directly to the quality of his athleticism. Abdul-Jabbar was still playing at 41, an age when most players are well into their second career. As a result, some people, factoring in the hectic pace of action on a basketball court, consider him to be the greatest athlete in the history of organized athletic competition. Indeed, after the Los Angeles Lakers won back-to-back titles in 1986–87 and 1987–88, Abdul-Jabbar played in his record twentieth season in the NBA. Previously, no one had ever played for eighteen seasons. During his career, Abdul-Jabbar was named to the All-Star Team 18 times, the All-Defensive Team 11 times, and on six different occasions, he was the league's Most Valuable Player.

Born in New York in 1947 as Lew Alcindor, he first made national news by leading Power Memorial High School to a 95–6 record, including 71 straight victories. At UCLA, he scored 33 points per game as a freshman, and each of the

next three years led the Bruins to the NCAA championship, winning the tournament MVP award all three times. After leaving an 88–2 record in his wake, Abdul-Jabbar was drafted by the Milwaukee Bucks in 1969. In six years with Milwaukee, Abdul-Jabbar led the league in scoring twice and averaged better than 30 points per game. Then, in 1975, the Los Angeles Lakers parted with Elmore Smith, Brian Winters, Dave Meyers, and Junior Bridgeman in exchange for Abdul-Jabbar and Walt Wesley.

After winning one league title in 1970–71 with Milwaukee, Abdul-Jabbar added a handful of championship banners in the 1980s, with the help of Magic Johnson. Abdul-Jabbar's consistency over time has been nothing short of phenomenal. During the 1987 playoffs, he failed to score in double figures against the Denver Nuggets, the first time he had missed in 467 consecutive games. In that season's final game, Abdul-Jabbar proved he could still dominate, scoring a season-high 32 points in the sixth and final game of the NBA championship series against Boston.

Although Abdul-Jabbar, the most dominant big man of his era, killed them softly with his velvet inside moves, often his incredible strength shined as brightly as his skills.

RED
AUERBACH

Disregard the campy, poised-to-whistle shot. Red Auerbach was always on the ball on the Boston bench.

Celtics Pride, one of the great intangibles in sport, is not so hard to explain. In truth, it stems from one source: Arnold Jacob Auerbach. "Let's face it," says former Celtic Gene Conley, "Red *is* the Celtics." And Conley isn't merely blowing the kind of smoke one sees emanating from Auerbach's omnipresent victory cigar.

Born in Brooklyn, New York in 1917, Auerbach was never much of a player. He averaged about 6 points per game as a 5-foot-10 guard at Seth Low Junior College and George Washington University. Coaching, however, was another matter. In the NBA's initial season, 1946–47, Auerbach's Washington Capitols posted a league-best 49–11 record. After stops at Tri-Cities and Duke University, Auerbach, then thirty-four, took over in Boston.

Before he arrived in 1950, the Celtics had compiled a dismal four-year record of 89–157; at home it was a troubling 54–55. Auerbach's first season there was a modest one. The Celtics won nine more games than they lost, but the record in Boston Garden was a phenomenal 26–6. That he achieved this with a dearth of player talent testifies to his attention to detail and a sensitivity that extended beyond the court.

"In the early 1940s, when I was in the Navy, I met Phil Rizzuto and we talked about the way Joe McCarthy managed those great Yankee clubs," Auerbach says. "Phil told me how Joe would take rookies from the farms and teach them little things like tipping properly in restaurants and acting properly in hotel lobbies. Joe was vitally concerned with the image of the Yankees. He believed the way you acted off the field had a great deal to do with the way you performed on it.

"I decided that any club I ever coached would be imbued with this philosophy: Dress like a champion, act like a champion, and you'll play like a champion. Celtics Pride was no myth, no fairy tale, but pride was only a part of what made us what we were. For a player to feel good about his

(right) Auerbach went out on top of the basketball world when his Celtics beat the Los Angeles Lakers for their eighth straight NBA title in 1966.

team and teammates, he must also feel good about his role in the team's success."

This explains why the Celtics are traditionally the NBA's most unselfish team, why despite sixteen championship banners, no Celtics player has ever led the league in scoring. Of course, it helps to have good athletes and Auerbach was unmatched in his ability to appraise and secure talent. In 1956, Auerbach made the deal of his life, trading away established stars Ed Macauley and Cliff Hagan for the rights to University of San Francisco center Bill Russell. Surrounded by players like Bob Cousy and Bill Sharman, Russell flourished as a rookie and led the Celtics to their first title.

The names changed with the years—Tom Heinsohn, Frank Ramsey, Jim Loscutoff, K.C. Jones, Sam Jones, and John Havlicek all made significant contributions—but Auerbach's success never abated. The Celtics delivered nine titles in ten years for Auerbach, an accomplishment unparalleled in professional sports history. The last came in 1965–66, leaving Auerbach with a twenty-year coaching record of 1,037 victories (an NBA record) and 548 losses— a .654 winning percentage. As Boston's president and general manager, Auerbach gave the Celtics a continued edge. He drafted Larry Bird as a junior-eligible, convinced Danny Ainge that basketball, not baseball, was his calling, and made one-sided deals for Dennis Johnson, Kevin McHale, and Robert Parish. It was no accident, then, that after Auerbach moved upstairs, Boston won titles under four different coaches. That's because Auerbach, the living definition of Celtics Pride, was still calling the shots.

RICK
BARRY

© UPI/Bettmann NewsPhotos

Some people, admittedly a minority among hoopologists, will tell you that Richard Francis Dennis Barry III was the greatest forward in the history of professional basketball. Certainly, the case can be made. Barry, a versatile 6-foot-8, appeared just as comfortable shooting his soft-as-silk jumper from the outside as he did muscularly driving through traffic to the basket. He could rebound and pass, too, no small feat for a man who scored 25,279 points in his fourteen-year career and averaged nearly 25 points per game in 1,020 regular-season games.

Still, when the great ones are recalled Barry's name is often bypassed. Why? Probably because Barry was a player whose style overshadowed his considerable substance. He scowled most of the time and seemed perpetually at odds with the referees, opponents, teammates, and even himself.

"I can honestly say there's never been a game I've played that I was totally happy with," Barry says. "Yet it's ironic that being such a perfectionist, I'm also a realist. I knew that it was impossible to play a perfect game, yet being the perfectionist that I am I always strived to play it, knowing full well that I never could.

"I was watching a Celtics-Lakers game and noticed the look on Magic Johnson's face during the last few minutes. He was so intense. He had something to prove. He was still playing with that effervescent quality, but you didn't see it in his face. That's the way I was when I played. That doesn't mean I didn't have a good time."

Born in Elizabeth, New Jersey in 1944, Barry led the nation in scoring as a senior at the University of Miami during the 1964–65 season with 37.4 points a game. The San Francisco Warriors made him the second pick of the draft and Barry responded with a Rookie-of-the-Year season that included 25.7 points and 10.6 rebounds per game. The following year, Barry ended Wilt Chamberlain's seven-year scoring dominance with a 35.6-point average that has been surpassed only by Chamberlain, Elgin Baylor, and Michael Jordan. And when Barry jumped to the American

There was nothing beatific about Rick Barry's on-court manner—he looked as intense as he played. His 90 percent freethrow average was testament to that.

© Manny Rubio

Basketball Association, giving the new league enormous credibility, he lost the respect of many NBA traditionalists.

He averaged 30 points per game over four seasons in Oakland, Washington, and New York before a court-mandated return to the NBA and the Warriors. A year later, in 1974–75, Barry averaged 30.6 points, nearly 6 rebounds, 6 assists, and 3 steals per game and led the Warriors to a stunning four-game sweep of the Washington

Bullets in the championship series. Barry made 101 of 110 freethrows during the playoffs, and finished his career as the NBA's leading freethrow shooter, with 90 percent.

Today, Barry sounds a little wistful when he talks about his playing days. "When people ask me the question 'Do you miss playing?' My standard answer is 'No.' But I have to add 'No, only because I don't think about it.' If I were to think about it, I would feel terrible."

E L G I N
B A Y L O R

© Long Photography

elgin Gay Baylor exerted such magnificent control over his 6-foot-5, 225-pound body, that it allowed him to release shots from almost any angle and collect rebounds with uncanny frequency. When he retired on November 4, 1971, after thirteen seasons, Baylor left the Los Angeles Lakers as the NBA's third-leading all-time scorer (23,149 points) and fifth-leading rebounder (11,463).

"I hoped to end my career after one last, successful season," Baylor said that day. "Out of fairness to the fans, to the Lakers, and to myself, I've always wanted to perform on the court up to the level and up to the standards I have established throughout my career. I do not want to prolong my career when I can't maintain those standards."

Playing basketball was not always Baylor's calling. In 1954, at the age of twenty, he was recruited out of Washington, D.C. as a football end by the College of Idaho. When football practice was canceled one day in Caldwell because of rain, the coach moved the workout into the gymnasium. Afterward, Baylor started throwing down some incredible baskets in a pickup game. Recognizing his ability, the football coach, who was also the basketball coach, quickly explained to Baylor that his football career was over. Baylor eventually transferred to Seattle University, where he led all Division I rebounders as a senior, averaging 19 rebounds and 31 points per game.

In 1958, the Minneapolis Lakers offered Baylor a $20,000 contract, and though he was six credits short of his degree in physical education, he leaped at the chance. Baylor scored 25 points in his debut and was honored as the NBA's Rookie of the Year in 1959. Not much more than

Elgin Baylor never met a shot he couldn't make. Here, he demonstrates the soft jump shot (left), and the running layup (right), through a pair of Boston Celtics. Baylor's feel for the basket resulted in 23,149 points, the NBA's third-best total.

© Naismith Memorial Basketball Hall of Fame

a year later, he broke Joe Fulk's long-standing record of 63 points for one game with 64. In 1960, Baylor lit up the New York Knicks for 71 points, an NBA record at that time. Two years later in the playoffs, Baylor singed the Boston Celtics for 61 points, a playoff mark that stood for twenty-two years before Michael Jordan threw down 63 against, oddly enough, the Celtics. In 134 playoff games, Baylor was at his best, averaging 27 points per game, second only to teammate Jerry West.

"Elgin was bull-strong, quick, and very daring," says West, a fellow Hall-of-Famer. "I think he was the most spectacular shooter the game has ever known."

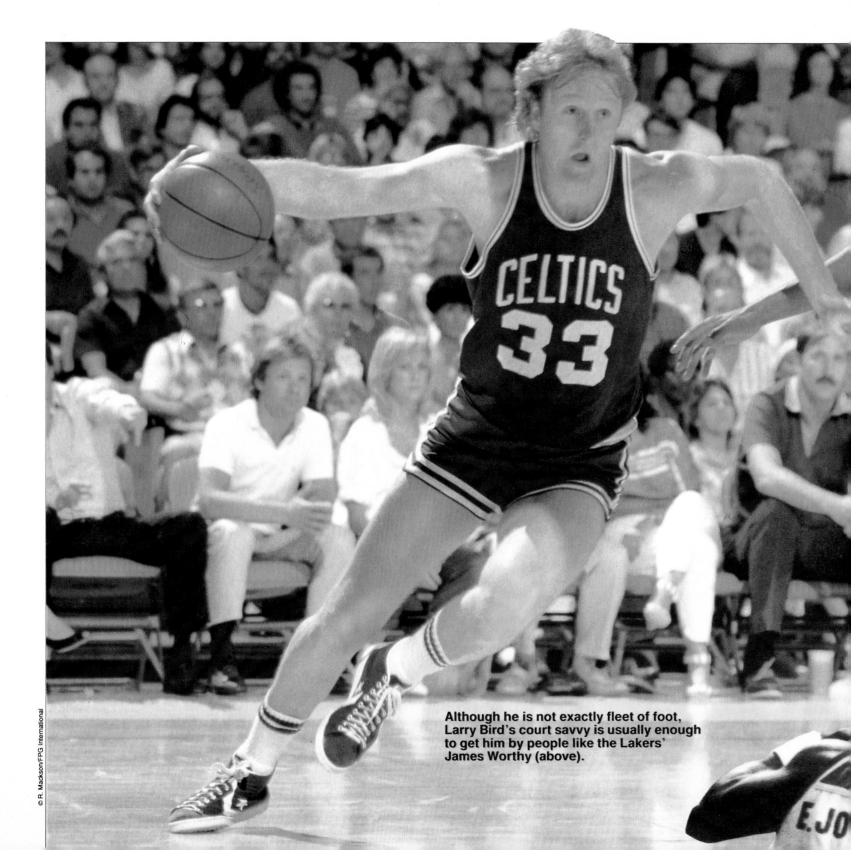

Although he is not exactly fleet of foot, Larry Bird's court savvy is usually enough to get him by people like the Lakers' James Worthy (above).

LARRY
BIRD

red Auerbach, the National Basketball Association's prevailing genius for more than 40 years now, stood up at a charity dinner a few years ago and said, "If I had to start a team, the one guy in all of history I would take would be Larry Bird. This is the greatest ballplayer who ever played the game." Just like that, the man who coached Bill Russell, Bob Cousy, and John Havlicek, and saw Wilt Chamberlain, Oscar Robertson, Julius Erving, Kareem Abdul-Jabbar, and Magic Johnson in their prime, pronounced Larry Joe Bird as the best ever.

It is an arguable point, to be sure, but rarely has there been a basketball player—or an athlete in any sport—with Bird's instinct for the game. His court sense was nearly omniscient. Teammates and opponents will tell you that the perfectly proportioned 6-foot-9, 220-pound forward had to be seen up close to be completely appreciated. Bird himself says that there were times when, out of boredom, he would try a more difficult shot or pass. Bird's command came from years of hard work in the gym.

"You've got to understand," he says. "My whole life's been basketball. It was never a recreation for me. It was something I fell in love with."

Bird was born in French Lick, Indiana (pop. 2,265), in 1956 and, encouraged by a $20 prize offered by his father, made the Springs Valley freshman team. Four years later, Bird arrived at Indiana University, but the large Bloomington campus intimidated him. He transferred to Indiana State, and in three years the Sycamores compiled a 81–13 record. Bird carried Indiana State to the 1979 championship game, but Magic Johnson and a deeper Michigan State team were too much.

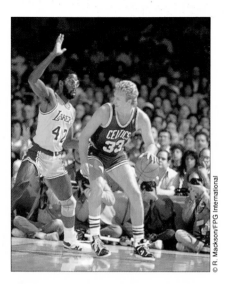

© R. Mackson/FPG International

Because Auerbach had drafted Bird sixth overall as a junior eligible in 1978, the Celtics turned their franchise around the next season. In 1978–79 the record was 29–53, the second-worst in the NBA. A year later, with Bird averaging 21 points and 10 rebounds a game, Boston produced the league's best record, 62–21. Since then the Celtics have won three championships and never suffered a losing month, a remarkable piece of consistency.

Individually, Bird won three consecutive Most Valuable Player Awards, in 1984, 1985, and 1986—something only Chamberlain and Russell had ever achieved. He was the playoff MVP in 1984 and 1986. In thirteen seasons, Bird's game was always well-rounded; when he retired after the 1991–92 season with a chronically aching back, he had averaged 24.3 points, 10.0 rebounds, 6.3 assists and 1.7 steals per game. He also led the NBA in free throw percentage in 1984, 1986 and 1987. That last season marked the first time a player ever shot 50 percent from the field and 90 percent from the free-throw line. It is the titles, however, that mean the most to Bird.

"That's why I play," he says. "I'm just greedy on them things. Winning the championship—I've never felt that way any other time, no matter how big some other game was. I remember the first time we won, against Houston [in 1981]. We were way ahead at the end, and so I came out with three minutes left, and my heart was pounding so on the bench, I thought it would jump out of my chest. You know what you feel? You just want everything to stop and stay like that forever."

The impact that Larry Bird has on the Boston Celtics is astonishing: After he arrived in 1979, the Celtics recorded a winning mark of sixty-one consecutive months. When he was sidelined for most of the 1989 season with a bone-spur disorder, the Celtics' streak ended abruptly.

© R. Mackson/FPG International

BILL
BRADLEY

© Naismith Memorial Basketball Hall of Fame

forget the statistics. Results are what count, and William Warren Bradley has achieved his share over the years. Many people believe the U.S. senator from New Jersey will one day be president. Look at his the-best-and-the-brightest resume so far: Member of the 1964 gold medal–winning U.S. basketball team in Tokyo, 1964 and 1965 College Player of the Year, Rhodes Scholar, Princeton University and Oxford University graduate, 1967 Sullivan Award, member of the New York Knicks NBA championship teams in 1970 and 1973. And since 1979, he has been a member of the U.S. Senate, too.

Bradley was never a big man (6-foot-5, 210 pounds) by NBA standards, but he was smart, worked terribly hard, and saw the big picture. He was born in 1943 in Crystal City, Missouri and was playing basketball by the age of nine. He was never particularly fast or blessed with leaping ability, but Bradley practiced three hours a day, working on his shot, boxing out, and passing—the fundamentals. At Princeton, Bradley averaged 30 points and 12 rebounds per game. When the Knicks drafted him in the first round of the 1965 draft, he politely declined the big contract and pursued his education in England. Along the way, he played for such basketball giants as Milan Simmenthal of the Italian Basketball League and the Oxford Five.

Bradley eventually joined the Knicks in 1967 and struggled through his rookie season. But soon there were signs that his game was just what the Knicks needed. Already blessed with center Willis Reed and guard Walt Frazier, New York employed Bradley as an all-purpose forward. Though he averaged only 12 points per game, Bradley

© Sue Cassidy Clark/FPG International

Though intelligence is often an underrated factor in professional sports, it was Bill Bradley's chief asset. Here, he uses it to turn the corner on the Lakers' Wilt Chamberlain (far left) and against the Cleveland Cavaliers (left) as he dishes the ball to a teammate with studied nonchalance. Later, he brought his cerebral game to the political arena, where his style and unselfishness again carried him toward the top.

could usually be counted on for the clutch basket. His rebound and assist totals were generally modest, but they came at important times. Reed and Frazier say today that Bradley was the glue that held those two championship teams together. He was unselfish and the chief reason the Knicks emerged as the league's best team.

Even as Bradley was scoring his 10,439 career points over ten seasons, he was preparing for his next career. He campaigned for Democratic candidates, worked at the Office of Economic Opportunity in Washington, D.C., and learned the political ropes. Bradley retired from basketball after an April 10, 1977 game at Detroit, and twenty-one months later was a U.S. senator. He was named Outstanding Freshman and his colleagues made him the chairman of a Democratic committee that would plot the party's economic course. While still in his first term, Bradley became the senior senator from New Jersey. Today he is still working hard, forging coalitions and improving himself and the people he works with. Bradley is a respected man with the ambition and ability (a rare combination in presidential candidates) to make it work on a national level.

Wilt Chamberlain, a 7-foot-1 giant of a man, sometimes stooped to conquer.

WILT
CHAMBERLAIN

© Naismith Memorial Basketball Hall of Fame

Wilton Norman Chamberlain brought a new dimension to the basketball court when he arrived in 1959. "I don't know what's going to become of this game with Chamberlain in it," said Dolph Schayes after witnessing a Chamberlain exhibition against NBA stars. "This guy is just fantastic."

Chamberlain, playing less than half of the benefit game, scored 20 points, pulled down 14 rebounds and blocked 10 shots, moving Syracuse's Al Bianchi to ask teammate Larry Costello, "Who needs him in the league? What's going to happen to us little guys? With him in there goaltending, we'll never be able to get a layup." Bianchi and Costello, a pair of 6-footers, weren't the only ones concerned after Chamberlain left the Harlem Globetrotters to play in the NBA. Chamberlain, at 7-foot-1, 275 pounds, was the most dominant player the league had ever seen. (Kareem Abdul-Jabbar broke Wilt the Stilt's all-time scoring record of 31,419 points in 1984, but needed many more games than Chamberlain to achieve that milestone.)

Born in 1936, Chamberlain played basketball for Overbrook High School in Philadelphia. Though he was infinitely more talented than most upperclassmen, Chamberlain was forced by NCAA rules to play for the freshman team his first year at the University of Kansas. Over the next two seasons, Chamberlain played with the varsity team. There he averaged 30 points and 18 rebounds a game before cashing in with the Globetrotters.

As Schayes had promised, Chamberlain was fantastic. To this day he holds many of the important NBA records. As a Philadelphia Warriors rookie, he won the scoring title, averaging 37.6 points a game, six more than Cincinnati's Jack Twyman. Chamberlain averaged three more rebounds than Boston's Bill Russell to win that celebrated matchup. And the amazing thing is, he got even better with age and experience.

The Stilt ripped down 55 rebounds against Boston in a 1960 game; scored 100 points on March 2, 1962 at Hershey, Pennsylvania; and singed Boston with 18 consecutive baskets a year later. Chamberlain led the NBA in scoring for seven straight years and was named its Most Valuable Player in 1960, 1966, 1967, and 1968. When he averaged 50.4 points per game in 1964, he became the only player to surpass 4,000 points in a single season. He led the league in rebounding eleven different seasons, playing for three different teams—Philadelphia, San Francisco, and Los Angeles. He won field-goal percentage honors nine times. And Chamberlain did it all with athletic muscularity and finesse that allowed him to operate almost unopposed under the basket.

Chamberlain was surprisingly versatile. Six years after scorching the nets with that 50.4-point scoring average, he led the league in assists, with 702. In 1971–72, he helped the Lakers to the NBA title (his second) in another way. While averaging only 14.8 points per game, Chamberlain led the league with more than 19 rebounds a contest, setting up baskets for Los Angeles' blazing guards, Gail Goodrich and Jerry West. And though he sometimes suffers by comparison to Russell's many championships, his record is outstanding. Clearly, Chamberlain was the giant of his time. Perhaps of all time.

B O B
COUSY

There was a time not so long ago that NBA athletes were regarded as something of a curiosity, and certainly not a group anyone would *pay* to see. In 1946–47, for instance, a mere 3,608 Celtics fans on average came out for each game at the Boston Garden. That was before Robert Joseph Cousy stepped into a green uniform in 1950.

While the NBA and the Celtics were struggling through their infancies, Cousy was honing the spectacular game that would help carry the league out of obscurity. He was born in 1928 in New York and like many boys his age found himself experimenting on the basketball courts in Queens. The coach at Andrew Jackson wasn't impressed, though: Cousy was cut from the freshman team because he was too short. The coach reconsidered, however, when he saw Cousy slice up the defense repeatedly in a neighborhood pickup game. By the time he reached Holy Cross College in 1947, Cousy had grown to only 6-foot-1, 175 pounds. What he lacked in size, however, he more than compensated for with creativity and peripheral vision; he always seemed to know the locations of all ten men on the court, which led to behind-the-back and over-the-shoulder passes so well conceived that they often surprised his teammates.

Holy Cross won the NCAA championship in 1947, and Cousy's individual game continued to grow over the next three years. Still, most NBA officials weren't sure if Cousy's game would translate to the professional level. The Celtics, in fact, passed on Cousy in the draft, opting instead for Charlie Share, a 7-footer from Bowling Green. Cousy was drafted by the Tri-City Hawks, then traded to the Chicago

Stags for Frank Brian. When the Stags folded a few months later, Cousy's name was placed in a hat, along with those of Andy Phillip and Max Zaslofsky. Celtics owner Walter Brown drew Cousy's name.

In his third season, Cousy led the NBA in assists (with 547) and was third in scoring with an average of 19.8 points per game. Just as important, the fans in Boston and around the league were warming to his flashy style of play.

Bob Cousy controlled the tempo of virtually every game he played for the Boston Celtics. Considering the caliber of his teammates, that is no small feat.

In Cousy's sixth season, the Celtics won their first NBA title and drew 10,517 fans per game, a record that stood for sixteen years. The addition of Bill Russell, Frank Ramsey, Bill Sharman, and Tom Heinsohn took some of the scoring pressure off of Cousy, but when the game was on the line, no one wanted the ball more.

In a 1953 playoff game, Cousy scored 50 points to beat Syracuse in four overtimes, sinking 30 of 32 free throws, including 18 in a row. Performances like that are why they still call Cousy "Mr. Basketball." He was named to ten consecutive All-Star teams, was a member of six world championship teams, and won the assist title eight times. In the end, that was the quality that made him great. Robert Joseph Cousy truly always gave of himself. Because of that unique ability, his teammates, fans, and the game were enhanced.

JULIUS ERVING

The legend of Julius Winfield Erving II began on the playgrounds in Roosevelt, Long Island where he first played basketball. Back then, they called him "Black Moses" or "Houdini." By the time he came to the NBA in 1976, Dr. J had already established himself as a unique presence. The legend had grown.

"Doc was the first guy to fly, he did things with a basketball nobody else had ever done," says Kevin Loughery, Erving's coach with the New York Nets of the American Basketball Association. "He had the biggest and the best hands in basketball. It was like he was playing with a grapefruit. I honestly believe that Doc did more for pro basketball than anybody, on or off the court. He wasn't just 'the franchise' with the Nets—he was the league. And he kept the league alive. Larry Bird, Magic Johnson, and Michael Jordan are great, but as far as handling every situation, on and off the court, Doc's the best."

Erving, 6-foot-7, 210 pounds, stretched the game vertically into a different dimension. He could actually take off at the free throw line, fifteen feet away from the basket, and throw down a slam dunk. He stretched the game intellectually, too, for here was a player who could eloquently read the Declara-

© Rick Stewart/AllSport

tion of Independence at Philadelphia's Fourth of July celebration, narrate *Peter and the Wolf* at the Philadelphia Zoo, as well as converse easily about the Equal Rights Amendment or the Civil Rights Movement. But as Los Angeles Lakers Coach Pat Riley once observed, "There have been *some* better people off the court, like a few mothers and the Pope. But there was only one Dr. J, the player."

Born in 1950, Erving played at the University of Massachusetts for three years, becoming only the seventh player in history to average more than 20 points and 20 rebounds over his college career. He eventually signed with the ABA's Virginia Squires as an undergraduate free agent. Erving was an instant sensation, scraping the roof of nearly every arena in which he played. In 1973, Erving was traded to New York, where he led the Nets to ABA championships in 1974 and 1976 and was named the young league's Most Valuable Player both years. Erving averaged 28.7 points per game over his five ABA seasons and was one of the primary reasons the NBA accepted four ABA franchises in 1976. Facing mounting financial woes, owner Roy Boe sold Erving to the Philadelphia 76ers, prompting general manager Pat Williams to note, "We got the Babe Ruth

Although Julius Erving did not invent the term hang time, he did seem to redefine the theory of gravity. Once he was airborne, opponents (like the Denver Nuggets, pictured here) weren't sure if he was going to pass or shoot.

© Photostaff/Allsport USA

of basketball.''

Erving averaged 22 points in eleven seasons with the 76ers, made the All-Star Team seven times and was the league's Most Valuable Player in 1981. Two years later, Erving led the 76ers to their first title in sixteen years. Yet more scintillating than the 30,000-plus points Erving scored over his career, was the style and grace with which they were delivered.

Rod Thorn, the NBA's vice president of operations and former Nets assistant coach, remembers a Nets fast break one night in San Antonio when Brian Taylor's bounce pass in front of Erving seemed on its way out of bounds. ''Doc just extended his right arm and caught the ball,'' Thorn said. ''But he never brought the ball into his body and never dribbled. In one motion, he just grabbed it, went up, and slammed it in. No other human could have done that.''

JOHN
HAVLICEK

It would be no great exaggeration to say that John Havlicek ran into NBA history, or that he began from an unusual place: The bench. As the Boston Celtics' famous sixth man, Havlicek recharged his team's batteries.

"Whether I start or come off the bench makes no difference to me," Havlicek said in 1968, by then a starter at the height of his career. "It doesn't change anything. Usually I came off the bench to get the confidence of the team and to get it running again—with a press, a steal, a long basket, anything. My game has always been to go as hard as I can, as long as I can. I want my opponent to chase me. I want him to get tired and loaf maybe once or twice on defense. That's when I'll take advantage of him by getting the cheap basket."

There's nothing cheap about running nonstop for thirty-five minutes a game, or averaging 20.8 points per game for sixteen seasons. Havlicek was not spectacular in any one phase of his game, but his shooting, rebounding, passing, and ball-handling skills made him one of the league's best swing men ever. At 6-foot-5, 205 pounds, Havlicek was barely big enough to survive the widebodies he played against at forward. And though he wasn't as quick as most of his counterparts at guard, more often than not Havlicek usually found a way to win.

Born in Martins Ferry, Ohio in 1940, Havlicek grew up playing football, basketball, and baseball at Bridgeport High School, and excelling at all three. During his senior season, Havlicek was an all-state quarterback and ultimately drew eighty college scholarship offers, most of them for football. Even Woody Hayes, the legendary gridi-

The Boston Celtics' John Havlicek is caught in a rare position—stationary—and in a more familiar pose, hassling an opponent. Although his non-stop game left both opponents and teammates breathless and amazed, he slowed down long enough in 1983 to let the Basketball Hall of Fame catch up with him.

© Manny Millan/Sports Illustrated

ron coach at Ohio State, wanted Havlicek to operate his offense. When Havlicek began to play a series of high school post-season all-star games, he became friendly with Jerry Lucas and Larry Siegfried. Together, they decided to attend Ohio State and play basketball.

In 1960, those players carried Ohio State to the NCAA championship. After starting for three years, Havlicek was taken in the seventh round of the 1962 draft by the Cleveland Browns of the National Football League. Turning down professional basketball offers from the Boston Celt-

ics and the Cleveland Pipers, Havlicek signed with the Browns and played a single exhibition game against the Pittsburgh Steelers as a wide receiver. He was cut one day later and quickly signed with the Celtics.

For four years, he was Red Auerbach's sixth man. In 1966, after the Celtics won three consecutive NBA titles, Auerbach moved him into the starting lineup. Boston then earned another championship banner and added four more over the next ten seasons. That gave Havlicek, the would-be football player, eight championship rings.

© R. Mackson/FPG International

Has a big man (6-foot-9) ever handled the basketball with as much skill as Magic Johnson? It's unlikely.

MAGIC
J O H N S O N

many players were fooled by Magic Johnson's terminally beatific manner, but his on-court smile was only a disguise for a ruthlessly competitive instinct. With the exception of Boston Celtics center Bill Russell, no other player in the history of basketball had such incredible success at such a young age. Johnson's basketball record is unimpeachable.

As a 6-foot-9, 220-pound freshman, Earvin Johnson, Jr., led Michigan State to its first Big Ten title in 19 years. One season later, their record was 26–6 and Michigan State won the NCAA tournament. Johnson was the Final Four Most Valuable Player, the first of three championships and MVP awards over a four-year span. Johnson, born in 1959 in Lansing, Michigan, left the Spartans in 1979 and joined the Los Angeles Lakers, who drafted him first overall with the pick they got from the Jazz as compensation for free agent Gail Goodrich. Johnson averaged 18 points and was among the league leaders in assists, with 7 per game. Once in the playoffs, Johnson played at another level, averaging 41 minutes and 18.3 points per game but adding 10 rebounds, nearly 10 assists, and 3 steals per contest. He was clearly the MVP of the final against the Philadelphia 76ers, the first rookie ever to win that award.

The Lakers were back in the final two years later and, again, Johnson raised the level of his game and won the MVP. All this by the age of 22. Before Johnson came to Los Angeles, the Lakers had won only one world title since the Minneapolis dynasty of the early 1950s. By the age of 29, Johnson had been the catalyst for five NBA titles in the 1980s and six titles overall, including the NCAAs. Russell, amazingly, had won six NBA titles by the age of 29, plus two NCAA championships and an Olympic gold medal.

In many ways, Johnson represented the new wave of NBA players who have nearly outgrown the court at its present dimensions. At 6-foot-9, Johnson had the size and strength to play center, as he did in the Lakers' successful 1980 championship round. At the same time, he played guard and had that rare peripheral vision that allowed him to lead the league in assists four times. When he retired at the age of 32 after the 1990–91 season, Johnson was the NBA's leading assist man, with 9,921, an average of 11.4 per game.

Sadly, Johnson's retirement overshadowed his greatness as a player. On November 7, 1991, Johnson announced to the sports world that he had contracted the human immunodeficiency virus (HIV), the virus that causes AIDS. Johnson left the Lakers to become an AIDS educator, but three months later he was drawn back to the All-Star Game when the fans voted him onto the roster. Naturally, Johnson was the MVP, scoring 25 points and adding nine assists, five rebounds, and two steals. Later, he was part of the U.S.A. "Dream Team" that took the men's basketball gold medal home at the Olympics in Barcelona, Spain, in 1992. Johnson had hoped to come back for the 1992–93 season, but opted to stay retired when the fears of some players were made public.

If he hadn't been so busy trying to distribute the ball to teammates, Johnson would probably have been a prolific scorer. In twelve NBA seasons he scored 17,239 regular-season points, an average of 19.7 points per game. That kind of versatility explains why Johnson is one of only three players—Wilt Chamberlain and Oscar Robertson are the others—to record 700 points, rebounds, and assists in a single season.

In 1987, Johnson put together the best season of his career, averaging 23.9 points, 12 assists, and 6 rebounds a game. He won the regular-season MVP award and, naturally, earned the playoff MVP as well, joining the select company of Jerry West, Willis Reed, Moses Malone, and Larry Bird. A year later, the Lakers became the first team to repeat as champions since the 1968–69 Boston Celtics. There was no other way to describe it but Magic.

© Brian Drake/SportsChrome Inc.

© Mitch Layton

Whether Michael Jordan is swooping in for another two points (left) or defying a Big Mac sandwich of Seattle's Xavier McDaniel and Nathaniel McMillan (inset), he *always* makes his presence known.

M I C H A E L
JORDAN

In 1986–87, Michael Jeffrey Jordan of the Chicago Bulls scorched the nets for 3,041 points—a record for guards in the National Basketball Association. He became only the second player in league history, after Wilt Chamberlain, to score more than 3,000 points over the regular season. The following year, Jordan was again the NBA's leading scorer, but here is what really makes Jordan such an imposing athlete: Not only was he named the league's Most Valuable Player, but Jordan was also honored as the Defensive Player of the Year.

Think about that contradiction for a minute. Jordan, at 6-foot-6, 198 pounds, was simultaneously recognized as the NBA's best offensive and defensive player. Though the defensive award is a recent phenomenon, it is safe to say that no player has ever been equally superior at both ends of the court in a single season. Chamberlain, even when he was winning seven consecutive scoring titles, was surpassed by Bill Russell on the defensive end. Oscar Robertson was a terrific all-around performer and Nate Archibald led the league in scoring and assists in 1973, but they both fell short of Jordan's marvelous example.

Coming into the 1987–88 season, Jordan had complained, correctly, that his offensive abilities overshadowed his defensive talents. In truth, he is the game's most spectacular player today, with an awesome arsenal of slam dunks and elusive moves around the basket. In addition to averaging 37.1 points per game in 1986–87, however, Jordan recorded 236 steals and 125 blocked shots, becoming the first player ever to produce 200 steals and 100 blocked shots in the same year. Then, Jordan went out and improved on history. His scoring fell off slightly, if you can call 2,868 points (35 per game) a decline, but his steals total (259) led the league and his 131 blocks were more than a handful of centers achieved. In one game against the New Jersey Nets, Jordan made 10 steals.

After eight seasons, including the 1991–92 campaign, Jordan had thrown up some incredible numbers. He had led the league in scoring six years in a row, compiling an average of 32.3 points per game, the highest in history. He was the NBA's MVP in 1988, 1991, and 1992, and led the Bulls to consecutive championships those final two years.

Another overlooked area is Jordan's durability. For a man who weighs less than most of the forwards and centers he meets in the congested lane, Jordan holds up remarkably well. In 1987–88, he appeared in all 82 regular-season games and led the NBA with 3,311 minutes played. In the next four seasons, Jordan missed only three games.

Born in Brooklyn, New York, in 1963, Jordan played high school basketball in Wilmington, North Carolina, where he was recruited by North Carolina Coach Dean Smith. As a freshman, Jordan helped lead the Tar Heels to the NCAA national championship, then won back-to-back College Player of the Year honors and an Olympic gold medal with the United States team in the Los Angeles Games of 1984. He later won another gold medal as a member of the U.S.A.'s "Dream Team" in 1992. On draft day 1984, the Houston Rockets made 7-foot Nigerian center Akeem "The Dream" Olajuwon the first overall pick, then the Portland Trailblazers also opted for size, taking 7-foot-1 center Sam Bowie. Jordan, the third choice, averaged 28 points per game and was easily Rookie of the Year in 1984–85. After missing 64 games of the following season with a foot injury, Jordan produced his two record-breaking seasons. And for his next trick? Jordan, a scratch golfer, says he's going to join the Professional Golfers Association Tour when he retires from basketball.

PETE
MARAVICH

The image of Peter Press Maravich that lingers is that of the shaggy-haired teenager careening down the basketball court in a baggy number forty-four Louisiana State University uniform, with floppy white socks—his lucky ones—sagging all the way. He was a wizard, a latter-day Bob Cousy blessed with rare court vision and an uncanny shooting touch. Maravich died suddenly in 1988, at the age of forty, but he left a legacy of brilliance, particularly in the college ranks, that quite possibly may never be matched.

Maravich dripped with charisma. Of course, he could score from any spot on the floor, but he could also get off an impossible behind-the-back pass at full speed or reach almost any rebound if he chose. He was a local legend in high schools in South Carolina and North Carolina before joining his father, Press, at LSU. Press had been a player in the old Basketball Association of America, the forerunner to the NBA, and knew his way around the court. As is the case with so many coaches' sons (Denver Broncos' quarterback John Elway comes to mind) Pistol Pete quickly developed into a dazzling performer. As a 6-foot-5, 200-pound freshman, Maravich appeared in seventeen games and averaged an astounding 43.6 points each time out. Granted, Maravich took 604 shots to make 273 baskets, a .45 percentage, but he wasn't afraid to shoot with the game on the line. As it turned out, his shooting percentage for that 1966–67 season was the best of his college career.

A year later, Maravich averaged 43.8 points over twenty-six games. In systematic fashion, Maravich raised the standard of his game as a junior and a senior, averaging 44.2 points, then 44.5 points each game. Never had the NCAA seen a talent like this. Maravich led the NCAA in scoring his last three years and set a variety of career records: Most points (3,667), highest scoring average (44.2), most games scoring at least 50 points (28), most

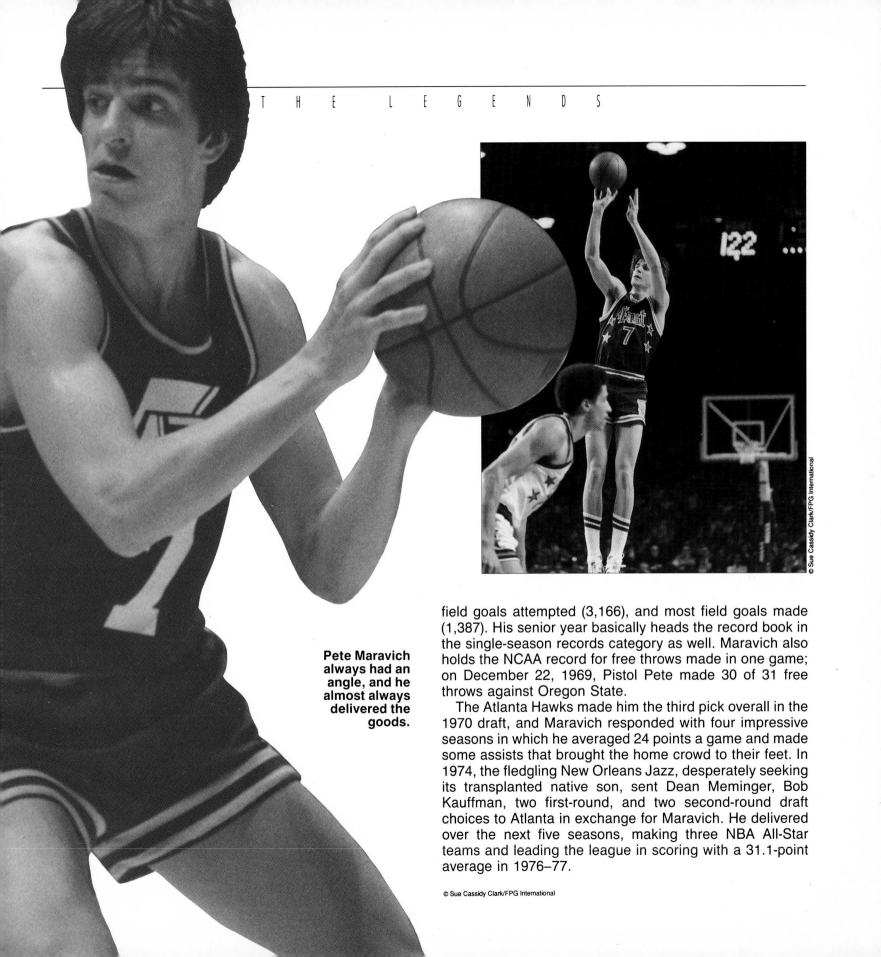

Pete Maravich always had an angle, and he almost always delivered the goods.

field goals attempted (3,166), and most field goals made (1,387). His senior year basically heads the record book in the single-season records category as well. Maravich also holds the NCAA record for free throws made in one game; on December 22, 1969, Pistol Pete made 30 of 31 free throws against Oregon State.

The Atlanta Hawks made him the third pick overall in the 1970 draft, and Maravich responded with four impressive seasons in which he averaged 24 points a game and made some assists that brought the home crowd to their feet. In 1974, the fledgling New Orleans Jazz, desperately seeking its transplanted native son, sent Dean Meminger, Bob Kauffman, two first-round, and two second-round draft choices to Atlanta in exchange for Maravich. He delivered over the next five seasons, making three NBA All-Star teams and leading the league in scoring with a 31.1-point average in 1976–77.

© Sue Cassidy Clark/FPG International

© Sue Cassidy Clark/FPG International

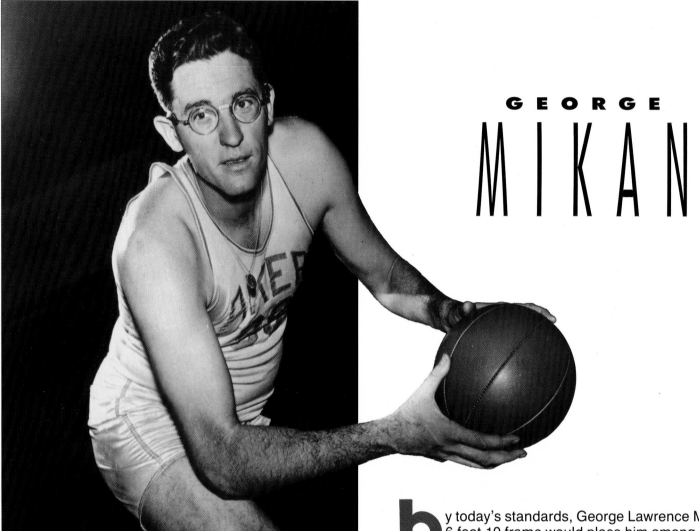

© Naismith Memorial Basketball Hall of Fame

GEORGE
MIKAN

b y today's standards, George Lawrence Mikan, Jr.'s 6-foot-10 frame would place him among the middle echelon of power forwards. Most NBA teams now have at least one 7-footer; the 1985–86 Milwaukee Bucks, for instance, had 7-foot-3 Randy Breuer as well as Alton Lister and Paul Mokeski, both 7 feet tall. Ralph Sampson, of the Golden State Warriors, is a 7-foot-4 forward. In 1942, however, Mikan's stature was an anomaly.

"We would set up a zone defense that had four men around the key and I guarded the basket," Mikan recalled later. "When the other team shot, I would just go up and tap it up."

Simple enough for a man with head and shoulders above most teammates and the opposition, but the NCAA de-

© AP/Wide World Photos

In his day, 6-foot-10 George Mikan was looked upon as something of an anomaly outside of the world of professional basketball. Inside that world, however, his height and build proved to be perfect for the sport.

cided a year later that this was an unfair advantage. And so, because of Mikan's towering presence, the course of the game was forever changed. The goaltending rule was introduced in 1944, prohibiting players from touching the ball once it was on its downward flight to the basket. But there was more to Mikan than 82 inches—he was named the greatest player in the first half-century by the Associated Press.

Born in Joliet, Illinois in 1924, Mikan's height as a freshman made him an obvious choice for the basketball team at Catholic High School, but Father Gilbert Burns noticed the gangly recruit was squinting. Convinced that an athlete of his couldn't wear glasses and play basketball at the same time, Burns cut Mikan from the team. He eventually learned the game at Quigley Prep in Chicago and moved on to DePaul, where Coach Ray Meyer polished the edges of his raw game. Mikan worked hard to develop a softer touch around the basket, which, combined with his 245-pound frame, proved devastating. Mikan was an All-American his last three years there and led the nation in scoring in 1944–45 and 1945–46. He scored 120 points in three games—53 against a Rhode Island team that triple-teamed him—to lead DePaul to the 1945 National Invitation Tournament.

The local entry in the National Basketball League, the Chicago American Gears, signed Mikan to a contract in 1946–47, and they promptly won the league title. Chicago then dropped out of the NBL and joined the Professional Basketball League of America, only to see it fold after eight games. He was eventually awarded to the NBL's Minneap-

olis franchise, which joined the NBA a year later.

Mikan surpassed previous NBA scoring leaders Joe Fulks of Philadelphia and Chicago's Max Zaslofsky with a 28.3-point average in 1948–49. He would be named to six consecutive All-Star teams and help the Lakers to five NBA championships in six years. Including his two NBL titles, Mikan was on seven championship teams in eight seasons. In nine professional seasons, Mikan averaged 22.6 points in 520 games.

Later, after an unsuccessful try at coaching, Mikan served as the first commissioner of the American Basketball Association and was responsible for the red-white-and-blue design of its ball. And despite what people said about his height, size was only one of George Mikan's virtues.

BOB
PETTIT

© Naismith Memorial Basketball Hall of Fame

Where does Bob Pettit fit in among the greatest basketball players of all time? At the very top, according to the experts who named him to the NBA's twenty-fifth and thirty-fifth anniversary All-Time Teams. After all, when he retired in 1965, Robert Lee Pettit, Jr., was the highest scorer in the history of professional basketball with 20,880 points, and third in rebounding with 12,849 boards. Don't underplay those rebounds—they say a lot about the 6-foot-9 athlete. "I recognize that I am totally prejudiced in behalf of Bob Pettit," Ben Kerner, owner of the St. Louis Hawks, once said. "He was a scoring champion, but more important, he was a tireless rebounder at both ends of the court."

Offensive rebounds, the kind that often require grit and an elbow or two, were just as much a part of Pettit's game as those wonderfully muscular drives to the basket. Born in Baton Rouge, Louisiana in 1932, Pettit was an All-American at the local high school before attending Louisiana State University in 1950. He was the Southeastern Conference Most Valuable Player his last three years, averaging 27.4 points and 14.6 rebounds over 69 games. Pettit was drafted by Milwaukee in the first round of the 1954 draft and won Rookie of the Year before the franchise shifted to St. Louis.

Pettit was selected to play in the All-Star Game as a rookie and made the First Team for ten consecutive years, a testament to his consistency. In 1956, Pettit won the Most Valuable Player award at the All-Star Game and repeated as the league's Most Valuable Player over the regular season, when he averaged 25.7 points and 16 rebounds a

game. Pettit led the NBA in scoring that year and again in 1959, (he had added the rebounding crown in 1956), but his greatest moment came in 1958 when he scored 50 points to beat the Boston Celtics in the sixth game of the NBA finals.

The Celtics had ripped through the Eastern Division,

Bob Pettit fought his way past two Cincinnati Royals during this 1957 game (right) on his way to another basket. When he retired in 1966 after eleven seasons, Pettit was the NBA's leading scorer, with 20,880 points.

winning 49 games and losing 23, compared to the Hawks' modest 41–31 record. The series opened with a Hawks victory over the Celtics in Boston and the two teams eventually split the first four games. After St. Louis won the fifth game in Boston, 102–100, the series returned to St. Louis. The Hawks, who had lost to the Celtics in the seventh game of the championship series in an excruciating double-overtime contest the previous year, had something to prove.

Pettit simply wouldn't let the Hawks lose, scoring 50 points—including 19 of St. Louis' final 21 points—when Boston mounted a spirited charge in the fourth quarter. The Hawks won, 110 to 109 and Pettit had set a new standard for field goals in a playoff quarter, with 8.

"It was the highlight of my career," says Pettit, now a successful banker based in New Orleans. "Of all the games I played, that championship meant the most to me. It still does."

OSCAR
ROBERTSON

The basketball always seemed to belong in Oscar Palmer Robertson's considerable hands. In them, it was a deadly weapon, for the "Big O" could kill you softly with infinite variety. Robertson, at 6-foot-5, 220 pounds, had the muscle to take the ball inside and the speed to beat his man, which allowed him to set that soft jumper in motion. As soon as he saw the double team, the ball would be gone, already in the hands of a teammate for another easy basket. In all of basketball their may never have been a man so consistently adept at both scoring and passing.

When Robertson broke into the NBA in 1960, the Celtics' Bob Cousy, himself one of history's most versatile players, observed, "Robertson is the best of his kind ever to come into the league." Today, it's still true. The numbers continue to stagger.

Through fourteen seasons, with Cincinnati and Milwaukee, Robertson amassed 26,710 points in 1,040 games, for an average of 25.7 per outing. Robertson led the league in assists six different times in a span of nine years, compiling a total of 9,887, or 9.5 a game. Throw in 7,804 rebounds, innumerable steals (they didn't start to keep track of them until 1973), and nine playoff berths, and it adds up to one of the most well-rounded careers in the history of the game. Robertson's fluid style was on display in the All-Star Game through the first twelve years of his career. He was the Most Valuable Player in three classics and holds the record for most points, 246, an average of more than 20 each time out.

Born in Charlotte, Tennessee in 1938, Robertson learned his control of the basketball at an early age in Indianapolis. He led Crispus Attucks High School to two state titles and was the Indiana Player of the Year in 1956 as a senior. At the University of Cincinnati, Big O averaged 33.8 points over four seasons and achieved a rare triple. In his last three years, Robertson's averages of 35.1, 32.6, 33.7 points per game led the nation and resulted in three consecutive College Player of the Year awards. Robertson held the all-time collegiate scoring record until the time of Pete Maravich. In 1959, Robertson was a driving force behind the Pan American Games gold medal–winning basketball team and one year later he was the co-captain of the United States team that won the Olympic basketball gold medal in Rome.

Robertson averaged 30.5 points per game as a rookie with Cincinnati, placing third in scoring behind Chamberlain and Baylor, and led the league in assists. For obvious reasons, there was no other choice for Rookie of the Year. After ten terrific seasons with the Royals, Robertson was dealt to Milwaukee, where he led the Bucks in assists, most of which were passes to a young Kareem Abdul-Jabbar. With that first-year combination, the Bucks won the NBA title in 1971.

Recently, Magic Johnson has focused new attention on the so-called triple double. It refers to the rare achievement of double figures in points, rebounds, and assists in a single game. Over one incredible season, 1961–62, Robertson averaged the triple double: 30.8 points, 12.5 rebounds, and 11.4 assists. It is quite possible that will never happen again.

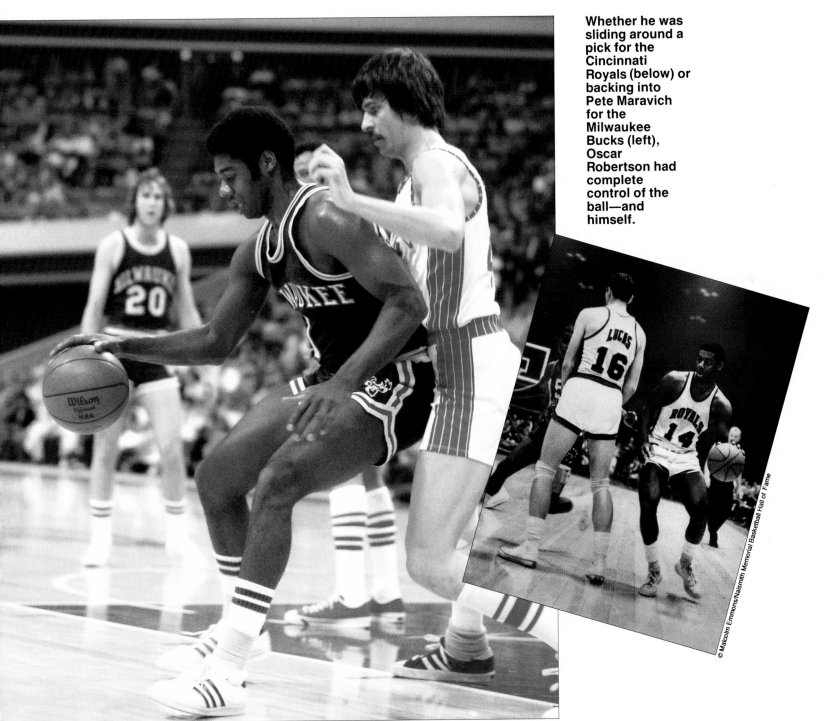

Whether he was sliding around a pick for the Cincinnati Royals (below) or backing into Pete Maravich for the Milwaukee Bucks (left), Oscar Robertson had complete control of the ball—and himself.

© Manny Rubio

© Malcolm Emmons/Naismith Memorial Basketball Hall of Fame

ADOLPH
RUPP

a dolph Frederick Rupp was there when basketball began—well, almost. He might have been, for he played under legendary University of Kansas coach Dr. Forrest C. "Phog" Allen and studied with Dr. James A. Naismith, a member of the Kansas faculty. Naismith, of course, invented the game of basketball, and Allen coached it better than anyone, winning 771 games. And then Rupp came along and won 875 games in forty-two years at the University of Kentucky. It is the standard against which all collegiate coaches are measured; to this day, Rupp and Allen are first and second on the all-time coaching list.

He was born in 1901 in Halstead, Kansas to immigrant parents from Austria and Germany. Rupp, the story goes, was shooting a homemade basketball through a barrel hoop nailed to a barn door by the age of five or six. He grew into a sound player and led Halstead High School in scoring his last two seasons. At Kansas, Rupp developed a deep understanding of the game from observation of Allen's methods and long conversations with Naismith. Coaching was the last thing on Rupp's mind when he graduated with a business degree. Wichita and Topeka, however, had little to offer at a time when the predepression economy was already winding down.

Rupp returned to school to pursue an advanced degree. He eventually landed a coaching job in Marshalltown, Iowa for wrestling, not basketball. Rupp bought a wrestling book and coached the team to the state championship. Later, he coached a Freeport, Illinois basketball team to a 67–16 record, and was named the Kentucky coach in 1930. His

Adolph Rupp (left) reacts from the bench as his Kentucky Wildcats beat the University of Mississippi in 1968 to push him past Phog Allen as the winningest college basketball coach in history.

starting salary was $2,800. There, his teams practiced disciplined fast breaks and tireless man-to-man defense. Before Rupp, Kentucky had enjoyed moderate success, winning 203 games and losing 142, but his winning touch was immediately evident.

Rupp's first team was 15–3, and over the first four years he compiled a 65–9 record. His legacy included those 879 victories and 190 defeats, for a winning percentage of .822, plus four NCAA titles, an NIT championship, and twenty-seven SEC titles. Rupp also produced twenty-five All-Americans and coached the U.S. Olympic team, (which featured five of his Kentucky Wildcats), that won the gold medal in 1948.

For the record, Rupp was not universally loved, despite his accomplishments. Rivals often viewed him as vain and vindictive, but nevertheless he was an institution in the state of Kentucky. Rupp died at the age of seventy-six in 1977, and even those who loved to hate him during his years of success at their expense were moved.

"He built a tradition of basketball known around the world for excellence and made us prouder to be Kentuckians," said Dr. Glynn Burke, who conducted the funeral services. "It's easy to be a nice guy. We live in a permissive society in which parents are afraid to discipline their children," Burke continued. "Coach Rupp never had that problem. And don't we always respect those teachers who demand the most of us? A friend is not just someone who says nice things all the time. It's someone who sees the best in us and wants to help us be what we want to be and what we can be."

© Walter Iooss Jr./Sports Illustrated

© Fred Roe

BILL
RUSSELL

above all, William F. Russell was a winner. Consider the following thirteen-month span as evidence: Led by the 6-foot-10, 220-pound center, the University of San Francisco completed a phenomenal fifty-six game winning streak by taking the 1956 NCAA championship for a second straight year. Then Russell anchored the U.S. Olympic basketball team that won a gold medal in Melbourne, Australia, after which he joined the Boston Celtics, who promptly won the first of sixteen NBA world championships in 1957, thanks in part to Russell's intimidating defense. That works out to three championships in just over a year.

The Celtics won eleven banners in Russell's thirteen seasons, including eight in a row. Coupled with his record at San Francisco, Russell won thirteen championships in fifteen years of basketball, a run of success that may never be equaled. Behind the numbers, however, is a player who revolutionized the game of basketball.

Even in the early days of the NBA, offense was the primary attraction and the standard against which most players were judged. Russell changed that. When Russell graduated from McClymonds (Louisiana) High School in 1952 and accepted a scholarship from San Francisco, he was already an expert shot blocker—adept at launching his lithe body through the air, and, with equisite timing, meeting the ball before it reached its zenith. Yet Russell didn't just swat the ball out of bounds. Over the years, he learned to tap it toward teammates, which led to countless fast-break baskets.

If opponents managed to take a shot, a miss was gener-

© Walter Iooss Jr./Sports Illustrated

The popular opinion on Bill Russell was that he couldn't score. Yet, although he was a defensive genius, over thirteen seasons, Russell managed to score 14,522 points. His presence helped the Boston Celtics win eleven NBA championships during his tenure.

ally a lost cause, for Russell was also an excellent re-bounder. This was obvious in his first year with the Celtics, when the league's highest-paid rookie led all players by averaging 19.6 rebounds per game. They didn't tabulate blocked shots in those days, or altered shots or intimidations either, but Russell was a ground-breaker in that respect, also.

The Celtics already had Bob Cousy, Bill Sharman, and Jim Loscutoff when Russell and Tom Heinsohn arrived in 1956, which gave Boston added scoring punch. Combined with their new defensive aggressiveness, the Celtics toughed out a seven-game championship series with the St. Louis Hawks that required two overtime periods in the final game.

Russell was never known as an offensive force, but with the Celtics' potent lineup he never had to push that facet of his game. Still, he averaged 15 points per game over his career, totaling 14,522. The basketball intelligencia never read much into Russell's offensive statistics, though. He was the league's Most Valuable Player five times—in 1958, 1961, 1962, 1963, and 1965—and an eleven-time All-Star. As a player-coach for three seasons, Russell led the Celtics to two titles before retiring in 1969. He finished with 21,721 rebounds, still second on the all-time list behind arch rival Wilt Chamberlain.

In terms of his individual dominance on defense and the unprecedented success of the teams he played for, Russell was without peer. In 1980, the Professional Basketball Writers of America named Russell the greatest player in the history of the NBA.

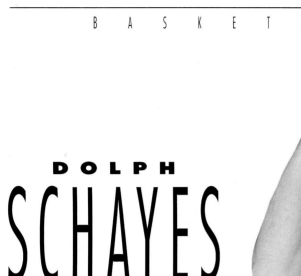

D O L P H
SCHAYES

adolph Schayes did not possess the scintillating moves of some of his contemporaries, such as Wilt Chamberlain, Oscar Robertson, or Bob Cousy. Persistence was his unique talent. Schayes, a 6-foot-8, 220-pound forward, missed one game because of a broken right wrist in 1952 and two years later suffered a fractured left wrist, but didn't sit out a game that time. Typically, Schayes saw those bad breaks as pluses to his career.

"Those were the best two breaks I ever had," he says. "They made me a better basketball player. When the right wrist went, I developed my left-handed shot. When the other one went, I had to take more care with my two-handed set shot. Because I was bothered by the cast, I had to rest the ball on my fingers and learned finger tip control. My advice to all young players is to break their wrists and develop the touch that casts make necessary."

Schayes was kidding, of course, but on the basketball court he was deadly serious. Born in New York in 1928, Schayes captained a successful high-school team at De-Witt Clinton in the Bronx. He was a sixteen-year-old freshman at New York University in 1945 and eventually earned All-America status in 1948 and was also awarded the Haggerty Award as New York's best college player. Schayes only averaged 10 points a game at NYU, but after turning professional at the age of twenty, he began to hone his style. Since he hadn't been forced to play center in college, Schayes had learned how to finesse bigger men, and how to move without the ball.

Schayes was never the dominant scorer in the manner of the Lakers' George Mikan, but he was consistent. The last

Note Dolph Schayes' flawless two-handed technique (rear left) at the freethrow line. Schayes was an old-school, New York basketball player whose all-around skills landed him a spot on the NBA's 25th Anniversary All-Time Team in 1971.

© Naismith Memorial Basketball Hall of Fame

of the two-handed set artists, Schayes practiced his shot for hours on end, aiming at a smaller basket within a basket that made it more difficult to score. He averaged 18 points a game in fifteen seasons with the Syracuse Nationals and appeared on the All-Star team twelve straight times. Schayes recorded 11,256 rebounds over his career and led the league in rebounds in 1951. On three different occasions Schayes was first in the NBA in free-throw percentage. When he retired in 1964, Schayes led the league in career scoring, with 19,249 points. In 1966, he was named Coach of the Year after turning a 40–40 Philadelphia team into a 55–25 contender.

In 1957, Schayes broke George Mikan's scoring record of 11,764 points. "I guess the basket I'll always remember was the one that broke the record," he said. "I wouldn't have wanted it to come on a foul or a tip-in or anything like that. It came just the way I hoped it would, on a long set shot. They stopped the game in Philadelphia and gave me the ball. I might as well enjoy the record while I have it, because Chamberlain is a cinch to break it in another five, six years." It happened, just as Schayes predicted, but it did little to diminish his place in basketball history.

JERRY WEST

They called him "Mr. Clutch." Jerome Alan West was, quite simply, the best player under pressure the game of basketball has ever known. To this day, West's 29.1-point average, forged in thirteen seasons of post-season play for the Los Angeles Lakers, is the highest playoff mark in history. In 1965 alone, his playoff average was better than 40 points each time out. For that matter, West's 27 points per game over fourteen years is the third best of all time, behind Wilt Chamberlain and Elgin Baylor. The 6-foot-2, 185-pounder stands as basketbal!'s greatest shooting guard.

West, born in Cheylan, West Virginia in 1938, first drew attention playing for East Bank High School, where he led his team to the 1956 state championship and averaged better than 32 points per game, becoming the first West Virginian to score more than 900 points in a high-school season. After high school, West chose to attend the University of West Virginia. Four years later he left Morgantown with twelve school records, a 24.8 points-per-game average, and two All-America honors. As a junior, West carried the team to the NCAA finals with a Most Valuable Player effort in 1959, the same year he was a member of the United States' gold medal–winning basketball team in the Pan American Games. A season later, West was co-captain of the Olympic gold-medal team in Rome.

The Minneapolis Lakers made him the second overall pick in the 1960 draft, then promptly moved to Los Angeles. There, West flourished as he gained confidence in his outside shot. In 1962, he was named to the first of his twelve NBA All-Star teams. Remarkably, West never

© Naismith Memorial Basketball Hall of Fame

seemed to slow down. In 1969, at thirty-one, he was the playoff Most Valuable Player in a losing effort against the Boston Celtics. A year later, West led the league in scoring with an average of 31.2. In 1972, his 747 assists were the most in the league as well. Through it all, West was a rugged defensive player, he was named to the All-Defensive team four times.

Jerry West's shot (far left) was a thing of beauty; here, he hoists one over the Knicks' Earl Monroe.

© Manny Rubio

After scoring 25,192 career points, West retired at the age of 36, yet he soon discovered basketball was a game he couldn't live without. "It seems very strange and frightening not to have that involvement," he said. "I miss it tremendously. It was an intimate part of my life...sitting around the day of the game at five o'clock, waiting, being nervous, thinking about it. No, I don't miss the roar of the crowd. That was part of my life that was so incredible words can't describe it. When I'm sixty and my kids are old enough to look back, I can open a scrapbook and say, 'Here's when I scored 30 points a game,' and I'll be very proud of that." Two years later, in 1976, West was named coach of the Lakers and promptly guided his former team to the best record in the NBA.

LYNETTE WOODARD

Thirty-eight years after Jackie Robinson broke the color barrier in baseball, Lynette Woodard broke the gender line with the Harlem Globetrotters.

© AP/Wide World Photos

lthough she made her most visible mark on history in 1985 as the first woman player in the Harlem Globetrotters' six-decade history, Lynette Woodard could really play the game of basketball. "Lynette was the first woman to be a college superstar," says her University of Kansas coach Miriam Washington. "If people had a chance to see her Kansas game films they'd be stunned. She led the nation in scoring, rebounding, steals ...she always led the nation in something."

This is true. Woodard, born in 1960, was discovered at Wichita North High School in Kansas by Washington, a former national team player. It was clear to the Kansas coach that "there was a young genius playing out there." At 6-feet even, Woodard had the power and quickness to dominate the women's college game like no other player before her. In 139 career games, she scored a staggering 3,649 points for an average of 26.3 per contest. Not only was that the highest total ever by a woman, but among Division I players, it ranks second behind Pete Maravich's 3,667-point career output. Woodard added 1,734 rebounds (12.4) and shot 52.5 percent from the field to lead Kansas to three consecutive Big Eight basketball championships.

Three years later, Woodard, a small-scale Magic Johnson, captained the U.S. Olympic team that won the gold medal in Los Angeles. One year after that, the Globetrotters announced they were holding tryouts for the team's first woman player. For Woodard it was the answer to her prayers—and an answer to a letter she had written to her cousin, Geese Ausbie, a member of the celebrated troupe. Since the ninth grade, Woodard had been dreaming of

© John Iacono/Sports Illustrated

playing with the 'trotters and, while a sophomore at Kansas, she asked Ausbie for a letter of recommendation. No answer was forthcoming, but Woodard was among those prospects on hand in North Carolina, and she won the job, based not only on talent, but personality.

Woodard carried the torch brilliantly, and her fresh, open manner helped the Globetrotters' attendance climb dramatically. It also underlined an important fact: Women *could* play basketball with a style and verve all their own. After two years, Woodard had a falling out with the 'trotters and left for the Women's Italian Basketball League, the showcase for women. There she became an international hero of sorts, playing to sellout crowds. In the early 1980s, there was a basketball league for women in the United States, but it failed miserably. If there is a renaissance of women's professional basketball in America, Lynette Woodard will probably have something to do with it.

"I hope so," she says. "For me that's not a farfetched thought. That's my message to people: If you can dare to dream it, then it just might happen."

JOHN
WOODEN

at the Basketball Hall of Fame, John Robert Wooden holds a unique distinction: He is the only man to be enshrined there both as a player and a coach. Wooden was that good.

Wooden is primarily known for his coaching prowess, and rightfully so. Under his care, UCLA won ten NCAA titles from 1964 to 1975, an incredible streak of consistent excellence that was approached only by the Oklahoma State University wrestling teams of the 1930s and the University of Houston golf teams of the 1960s. Wooden's success was the result of years of hard work, both on and off the court.

Born in Martinsville, Indiana in 1910, Wooden's first taste of success came at an early age, as a player, not a coach. He was a three-time All-State basketball player at Martinsville High School in Indiana, and continued to excel in college also. At Purdue University Wooden was a three-time Helms All-American and captained the Boilermakers his last two seasons. As a senior, Wooden set a Big Ten scoring record and led Purdue to the national championship. For his efforts Wooden was named College Player of the Year. He then graduated to professional basketball and started for the Kautsky Grocers of Indianapolis, where he once made 138 consecutive free throws in competition. His astonishing coaching career was still to come.

Wooden coached at Dayton High School in Kentucky for two years, and another nine years were spent at Central High School in South Bend, Indiana compiling a record of 218–42 before joining the war effort. Upon his return in 1946, Wooden coached Indiana State Teachers' College to

© Naismith Memorial Basketball Hall of Fame

Although John Wooden is only sixth on the all-time list of winningest college coaches, there was a quality to his work. The Wizard of Westwood won ten NCAA titles in twelve seasons at UCLA.

a record of 47–14 over two seasons. In 1948, Wooden weighed two prospective offers, from the University of Minnesota and UCLA. He was waiting at home for a prearranged call from Minnesota when UCLA contacted him looking for an answer. He accepted the job on the West Coast grudgingly, unaware that phone lines in the upper midwest were down. Minnesota got through an hour too late. Wooden, however, wasn't thrilled with what he found in Los Angeles.

"I was the most discouraged person so far as basketball was concerned," Wooden says of the team that returned no starters from a 12–13 season. "It really looked bad." Yet, Wooden somehow turned his team around. The Bruins won their first six games, set a home-court winning standard of thirteen straight games, and finished with a 22–7 overall record.

Over the years, Wooden put together an organization that withstood the flux of players with a mere four-year tenure. Wooden established records that may never be broken: eighty-eight consecutive victories (the previous mark was sixty), ten NCAA titles (compared to previous best of four), seven consecutive titles (five more than the old record), thirty-eight straight NCAA tournament wins (the previous mark was thirteen), and eight undefeated conference championships. Wooden's lifetime coaching record was 905–203, 667 of those victories coming in the college ranks, leaving him sixth on the all-time list.

Wooden retired from coaching in 1975 after winning his tenth national title in twelve years. He left a void that will probably never by filled.

THE GREATEST GAMES

It might have been the greatest basketball game ever played — just don't look for it in the usual compilations of such events. On January 29, 1964, Boone Trail High School, of Mamers, North Carolina defeated Angier, North Carolina 56–54 in a game that took thirteen overtime periods. It was, quite naturally, the longest scholastic game ever played.

There are other, more familiar games that bear reinspection. Consider, if you will, the game in January 1988 when Rickey Green of the Utah Jazz threw in a long three-point shot and scored the NBA's 5-millionth point. Forty-two years earlier, the first points belonged to Ossie Schectman, a guard for the New York Knicks. He drove to the basket and scored early in the inaugural game of the Basketball Association of America against the Toronto Huskies, earning a unique place in history.

How about the sextuple-overtime game between the Rochester Royals and the Indianapolis Olympians in 1951? The Olympians won, 75–73, in a game that may never be equaled for the energy it drained from the participants. Or take the triple-overtime struggle between the Boston Celtics and Phoenix Suns in 1976. That it came in the fifth game of the championship series left many observers thinking it was the most exciting game in history. Two days later, the Celtics won their thirteenth title in twenty years, but the 128–126 fifth-game victory is the one people remember. History was also made on April 5, 1984, when Kareem Abdul-Jabbar of the Los Angeles Lakers dropped a hook shot from the right baseline in a game against the Utah Jazz. With that field goal, Abdul-Jabbar surpassed Wilt Chamberlain's scoring record of 31,419 points that was once thought to be unassailable.

In terms of importance, "The Game of the Century" may actually have lived up to its name. Played on January 20, 1968, it pitted two great college teams, UCLA and the University of Houston, led by two great stars, Lew Alcindor and Elvin Hayes. Houston won the game in a 71–69 upset and sparked the nation's love affair with college basketball. Said UCLA announcer Dick Enberg, "It was the first time someone really opened the jewel box and saw the diamond." Enjoy these basketball gems.

THE
FIRST
NBA GAME
New York Knicks 68, Toronto Huskies 66

NOVEMBER 1, 1946: Ossie Schectman learned basketball under one of the great coaches, Clair Bee, at Long Island University, and helped lead Bee's Blackbirds to win the National Invitational Tournament in 1939 and 1941. Afterwards, in the Army Air Corps, he played basketball virtually every day, honing his skills and increasing his knowledge of the game. Yet he could not have known that he would go on to score the first points in the history of the NBA.

After World War II, Schectman was approached by promoter Ned Irish. Would he be interested in joining a new enterprise called the Basketball Association of America? Informed that his annual salary would be $5,000, Schectman jumped at the chance. He didn't know that the BAA would eventually lead to the National Basketball Association and change the world's perception of the game forever.

The New York Knickerbockers, who claimed a gangly 6-foot-5 kid named Bud Palmer as their tallest player, traveled to Toronto for the new league's first game on November 1, 1946. A total of 7,090 spectators came out for that contest. After the jump at center—or was it a faceoff?—Leo Gottlieb, from Brownsville, Brooklyn, dribbled the ball up court and bounced a pass to Schectman, who laid the ball in for the first points in league history. "Of course I remember it," Schectman says. "It was a driving basket. We had a lot of local guys, and that was the style."

The Knicks would ultimately win 68–66 and finish the season with a 33–27 record, sixteen games behind the Washington Capitols and eleven ahead of the Toronto Huskies, who quickly disappeared from the league.

Schectman himself quickly exited. In an attempt to run down a loose ball one night in Chicago, he dove over a fallen Max Zaslofsky and caught a knee in the stomach. Schectman's small intestine was ruptured, and though he tried to come back later in the season, he was never quite the same.

The NBA, on the other hand, flourished quite nicely after Schectman's shot in the arm.

Courtesy Toronto Globe & Mail

Courtesy Toronto Globe & Mail

THE LOWEST SCORING GAME

Fort Wayne Pistons 19, Minneapolis Lakers 18

NOVEMBER 22, 1950: There was nothing to suggest that the Fort Wayne Pistons had much of a chance against the NBA champion Minneapolis Lakers when the two teams met on November 22, 1950. The Lakers had accumulated a 51–17 record the year before, and went nine for eleven in playoff games, defeating Syracuse for its second straight title under coach John Kundla. Not only were the Lakers headed toward a 44–24 record and another Western Division crown this year, but they won twenty-nine of thirty-two games at home that season. The Pistons, on the other hand, were scuffling. Their final mark would be 32–36, including an abysmal 5–27 count on the road.

The Pistons were painfully aware of this statistical baggage as they prepared for what should have been another blowout on the road. But, borrowing a technique from many teams before them, they made a decision to hold the ball as long as possible and only shoot when optimum opportunities presented themselves. Remember, this was before the league instituted a twenty-four-second clock, so there was no urgency to shoot the ball. In effect, Fort Wayne was shortening the game to give itself the best chance to win. And it worked.

The Pistons, judicious in their shot selection, led 8–7 after the first quarter, though the Lakers rallied to take a 13–11 halftime lead. Fort Wayne fought back to within 17–16 at the end of three periods and eventually won—19–18. Referees Jocko Collins and Stan Stutz called the game closely, whistling players for a total of 24 personal fouls. This determined the outcome, for each side was able to make only 4 field goals. In the end, Fort Wayne won

© Naismith Memorial Basketball Hall of Fame

George Mikan (far left) scored fifteen of the Lakers' eighteen points. Lakers' guard Slater Martin (left) missed all three of his freethrow attempts.

because it shot better from the freethrow line; Minneapolis was given 17 opportunities from the charity stripe and could only convert 10, while Fort Wayne was a more efficient 11 for 15.

Six-foot-ten center George Mikan, who would lead the league in scoring with a 28.4-point average, was stifled effectively. He scored all four Minneapolis baskets, going 4 for 11 from the field, but his teammates were a collective 0 for 7. Mikan was also 7 for 11 in free-throws, giving him a total of 15 points—3 fewer than the team total. Guard Slater Martin might have made a difference, but he missed all three shots from the foul line. On the other side, guard John Oldham was the leading scorer, with 5 points. Paul Armstrong scored 4 points and forward Fred Schaus (who was the team's top scorer then) and center Larry Foust scored 3 points each.

The Lakers averaged nearly 83 points a game on offense and Fort Wayne was working on an 84-points-per-game season. But for one night in Minneapolis, it was as if the score stood still.

THE
LONGEST
GAME

Indianapolis Olympians 75, Rochester Royals 73

JANUARY 6, 1951: In the early 1950s, professional basketball was struggling. Like football in its infancy, the pro game was secondary in interest to the college ranks. Seeking a marketable angle, the NBA introduced the twenty-four-second clock prior to the 1954–55 season, which made it mandatory to shoot the ball on each possession before the clock wound down, therefore speeding the game up, and, the owners hoped, making it more exciting. The experiment worked and changed the nature of the game. That is why there may never be another game like the one played between the Rochester Royals and Indianapolis Olympians on January 6, 1951.

"I doubt that it will ever happen again," says Red Holzman, who played seventy-six of the game's seventy-eight minutes. "The twenty-four-second clock forces a team to shoot, and don't forget, the shooters today are great. It's very tough for two teams to keep tying in overtime periods. Something has to give."

The longest game was decided in six overtime periods, as the Olympians won, 75–73. With 3,300 on hand at the Edgerton Sports Arena in Rochester, the Royals took to the floor riding a seven-game winning streak. The close-to-the-vest game was tied at 65 after regulation. Both sides had their share of good ballhandlers and chose disciplined styles of play. In fact, two of the overtime periods had no scoring at all because the team with the ball chose to hold it for one potentially winning shot. In one five-minute stanza there wasn't a single shot by either team.

Arnie Risen forced the game to a sixth extra period when he scored both of the Royals' baskets. Risen sandwiched a

© UPI/Bettmann NewsPhotos

layup around Alex Groza and a desperation hook shot around a field goal by Indianapolis' Ralph Beard. For nearly four minutes of the final period, Rochester carefully protected the ball, then called a timeout to discuss strategy with Coach Les Harrison. It backfired. The Olympians came out swarming on defense, forced two bad shots and

The Olympians take a bow: (from left to right) Wah Wah Jones, Cliff Barker, Alex Groza, and Ralph Beard.

Groza fired a rebound down the court to Beard, alone at the top of the key. After dribbling once, Beard threw up the game-winning twelve-foot shot that fell through the net with one second remaining.

"If there had been a twenty-four-second clock, the game never would have gone six overtimes," said Harrison. "In fact, our team, with Holzman, Davies, and Wanger, were all great ballhandlers and playmakers, and they were very much responsible for the advent of the twenty-four-second clock. Red could dribble the ball indefinitely."

Which is as good a reason as any that today's game is a run-and-gun affair.

© Neil Leifer/Sports Illustrated

THE
GAME
OF THE
CENTURY

Houston Cougars 71, UCLA Bruins 69

JANUARY 20, 1968: By the mid-1960s professional basketball had replaced the college version as the most popular form of the sport, thanks in part to the Wilt Chamberlain–Bill Russell epics and the highly skilled operators of the pro ranks. Today, college and professional basketball share equal popularity. What happened to warrant the change? Credit Guy V. Lewis, the man who conceived the idea for "The Game of the Century."

Lewis was the coach of the Houston Cougars. Following a loss to Oregon State in the Western Regionals of the 1966 National Collegiate Athletic Association held at UCLA's Pauley Pavilion, Lewis found himself thinking about the future. UCLA was excited about the prospect of Lew Alcindor at center and Houston had reason for optimism as well. "They obviously were going to have a great team and I felt we were going to be good, too, with Elvin [Hayes] and Don Chaney around for two more years," Lewis said. Despite the fact that Houston was playing out of a twenty-five hundred seat gym, he went and pitched the idea of a game between the two teams to athletic director Harry Fouke, suggesting a $10,000 guarantee for both teams and the Houston Astrodome as the site.

Eventually, Judge Roy Hofheinz, the owner of the Astros and operator of the Astrodome, consented as did UCLA coach John Wooden. The date would be January 20, 1968. The two teams met in the semifinals of the 1966–67 NCAA tournament, setting the stage for unprecedented interest. When it became clear the next season that UCLA, winner of three NCAA titles in four years, was the class of college basketball, both schools were deluged by ticket requests—

© AP/Wide World Photos

It was billed as a showdown between UCLA's Lew Alcindor, (far left, in blue) and Houston's jubilant Elvin Hayes (below). The Cougars prevailed, 71–69, largely because Hayes outscored Alcindor, 39 to 15.

© Neil Leifer/Sports Illustrated

for seats no closer to the court than forty yards. The media followed suit, making the matchup the most widely covered regular-season game in college history. UCLA came in with a forty-seven game winning streak, and Houston appeared to be the only team with a chance to beat the Bruins. "I didn't think we'd sell out the Dome," Lewis said, "but then the situation just worked out perfectly."

Wooden wasn't so sure. "I didn't think either team would play well," he says now. "There were lights for television directly above the baskets, and it was like playing out in a pasture, in a sense, because the floor was out in the middle of this enormous space. I remember that walking out from the dressing room, it was so far I didn't know when we would get to the court."

The crowd present was 52,693, the largest ever to see a basketball game indoors at the time. The 6-foot-9 Hayes blocked several of the 7-foot-2 Alcindor's shots and scored an incredible 29 points in the first half on 14-for-19 shooting, but the Cougars only led 46–43 at the half. The Bruins rallied to tie the score three separate times, the last at 69-all with forty-four seconds left. Two free throws by Hayes and two blunders by UCLA left the final score Houston 71, UCLA 69. Hayes finished with 39 points, 15 rebounds, and 8 blocked shots. Alcindor, who had suffered a scratched cornea a week earlier, was not himself, missing 14 of 18 shots and scoring only 15 points.

And so, college basketball was never the same. Al McGuire, a national basketball expert, observed, "It took the game out of the attics and into the main circles." It has remained there ever since.

THE TRIPLE OVERTIME GAME

Boston Celtics 128, Phoenix Suns 126

Just one different bounce of the ball on the rim, at any time, could have changed the outcome of this marathon game. At one point, referee Richie Powers had to restrain volatile Boston center Dave Cowens (far right).

JUNE 4, 1976: No one gave the Phoenix Suns much of a chance against the Boston Celtics in the 1975–76 NBA championship series. After all, the Suns had struggled to a 42–40 record over the regular season, good (or bad) for third in the five-team Pacific Division. The Celtics, meanwhile, had put together a 54–28 regular-season record and won ten of fifteen playoff games. Moreover, Boston had beaten the young Suns seven straight times over a two-season period. Still, Phoenix, starting rookies Alvan Adams and Ricky Sobers, had managed to scrape past Seattle and Golden State to the finals. Now they were going to give the Celtics the fight of their lives.

The Celtics easily won the first two games at Boston Garden, but Phoenix narrowly won the next two, setting up the pivotal fifth game in Boston on June 4. It was very nearly over before it was over. The Celtics outscored the Suns 32–12 in the game's opening nine minutes. At one point, the lead grew to 22 points, the largest of the game. Boston led 36–18 at the end of the first quarter, thanks largely to blistering 61 percent shooting. Phoenix cut the lead to 61–45 at halftime and worked it down to 68–64 with a third-quarter run. Nevertheless, Boston's 92–83 lead with 3:49 remaining in the game seemed secure.

Then Paul Westphal, a former Celtic and first-round draft choice, got hot. He scored 9 of the Suns' next 11 points and his 3-point play pulled Phoenix even at 94 with thirty-nine seconds left on the clock. Curtis Perry's free-throw gave the Suns a lead, but John Havlicek dropped in a foul shot of his own to send the game into overtime. Perry saved Phoenix in the first extra session with a turn-around

jumper and a baseline fall-away with forty-five seconds left. The second overtime had a little of everything: With the Suns trailing 109–106 with nineteen seconds left, Dick Van Arsdale scored his only basket of the game. Then Westphal stole a pass from Havlicek and passed it to Perry, who put Phoenix ahead 110–109. Havlicek responded with a running jump shot to give Boston a one-point lead. The crowd, thinking the game was over, exploded in celebration. But referee Richie Powers was under the impression there was one second left.

With the Suns down 111–110, Westphal quickly called a timeout, but drew a technical foul because none were left. Jo Jo White sank the free throw, giving the Celtics a two-point lead, but Westphal then took an inbounds pass and tied the score of 112–112, forcing a third overtime. White and Glenn McDonald, a third-stringer, combined for 12 points in that session and led the Celtics to a 128–126 victory.

When it was all over, Boston coach Tom Heinsohn had to be helped to the trainer's room, where he had passed out, suffering from nervous exhaustion. The Celtics locker room was, not surprisingly, a subdued place filled with drained athletes. Boston forward Paul Silas looked down at his shredded sneakers and mused, "Can these go one more game? Can I?" The answer to both questions was yes, and the Celtics won an anticlimactic sixth game, 87–80, to earn their thirteenth championship banner. Yet in all those years, rich in tradition and glory, there was never a game as exciting or well played as the triple-overtime contest with the Suns.

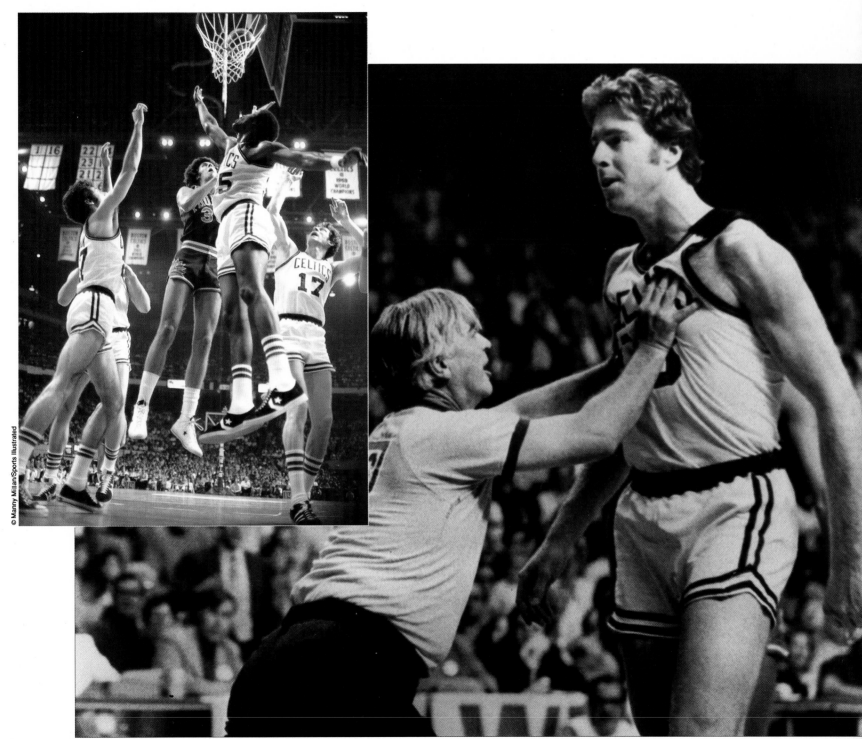

© Manny Millan/Sports Illustrated

© UPI/Bettmann NewsPhotos

While Michael Jordan is the center of the basketball universe, it is clear that he wouldn't have won a single National Basketball Association championship without Chicago's smooth forward Scottie Pippen.

THE
BULLS
R E P E A T

Bulls 97, Trail Blazers 93

JUNE 14, 1992: After Michael Jordan and the Chicago Bulls finally broke through and won the 1990–91 National Basketball Association championship, Jordan was asked if he thought his team could repeat as champion. "Can we repeat?" Jordan asked himself. "Well, yes. Will we? There are a lot of variables involved, so I can't make any promises. I don't know if I'll ever have the same feeling as I did last June when we beat the Lakers. The emotions people saw in me and my teammates were ones of hard work. I do know this: Now that I've tasted one championship, I definitely want another one." Said assistant coach Johnny Bach: "Only the Bulls can beat the Bulls."

Only the Boston Celtics, Los Angeles Lakers (most recently in 1988), and Detroit Pistons (1990) had managed to win back-to-back titles, so the Bulls' challenge was daunting indeed. The Bulls, powered by Jordan's ability to score at will, won 67 regular-season games and then struggled through two tough series, with New York and Cleveland, to reach the final and a series of dates with the Portland Trail Blazers.

AP/Wide World Photos

In Game Six of the 1992 NBA finals, which pitted the Bulls against the Portland Trail Blazers, 12 of Michael Jordan's game-high 33 points came in the fourth quarter.

Though the Bulls' success in 1991–92 was based on their new-found depth, Chicago was still basically a team comprised of Jordan and, as he sometimes liked to say, his "supporting cast." In Game One, he was astonishing, scoring a record 35 points in the first half alone. Six of Jordan's baskets were three-point efforts. Jordan coasted to a total of 39 and the Bulls rolled, 122–89, at Chicago Stadium. With the series tied at two games apiece, Jordan personally won Game Five in Portland. He scored 46 points in Chicago's 119–106 victory.

For the longest time, Game Six appeared to belong to Portland. The Bulls had lived dangerously all season long, notably in a seven-game series against the Knicks, and this game was no exception. As the fourth quarter opened at Chicago Stadium, the Bulls trailed the Trail Blazers 79–64 and looked to be quite dead. Jordan, who had scored only two points in the first quarter, was on the bench taking deep breaths. He had blown two layups in the third quarter and had another knocked away. So the Bulls sent out the unremarkable unit of B.J. Armstrong, Bobby Hansen, Stacey King, Scott Williams, and starter Scottie Pippen. Suddenly the Bulls were back in the game. They cut the margin to 79–70, then 81–78. Jordan came back well-rested and, with just over four minutes left, put Chicago ahead, 89–87, for the first time since early in the game with a layup. Twelve of Jordan's game-high 33 points came in that fourth quarter, including Chicago's last six. And so, the Bulls were champions again.

The Trail Blazers never really found a way to deal with Jordan. Even though they had Drexler, the league's acknowledged second-best player, guarding him on defense, Jordan averaged 35.8 points per game, the second-highest total ever in an NBA six-game series. "Going into the series, I though Michael had 2,000 moves," Drexler said. "I was wrong. He has 3,000."

KAREEM ABDUL-JABBAR BECOMES THE LEADING SCORER

© Fred Roe

APRIL 5, 1984: For years, the debate raged: Who was better, Wilt Chamberlain or Bill Russell? Chamberlain dominated the game at the offensive end, but Russell owned the defensive side. Russell retired in 1969, with a modest scoring average of 15.1 points per game, along with eleven championship rings. Chamberlain, who left in 1973, won only two titles but averaged 30.1 points in 1,045 career games and a monstrous total of 31,419 points.

But even as Chamberlain was putting the finishing touches on a record many thought would never be approached, a rookie center in Milwaukee was beginning his own professional career in 1969. Lew Alcindor placed second behind Chamberlain's Los Angeles Lakers teammate Jerry West in scoring that season, averaging 28.8 points per game. In the 1970–71 season, the renamed Abdul-Jabbar led the league in scoring, amassing 2,596 points, won the regular-season Most Valuable Player award, carried the Milwaukee Bucks to the NBA title, and was named Most Valuable Player of the championship series. He added another scoring title the following season (to go with another league Most Valuable Player), scoring a career-high 2,822 points for an average of 34.8.

Despite Abdul-Jabbar's instant impact, there were those who insisted that Chamberlain and Russell were by far the superior players; Chamberlain, for instance, enjoyed five seasons with a higher scoring average than Abdul-Jabbar's best. As time passed, however, Abdul-Jabbar proved he was in Chamberlain and Russell's league. For one thing, he ran the court better and, though he didn't possess Chamberlain's awesome scoring touch or intimi-

date like Russell did, Abdul-Jabbar proved to be a better shooter than either.

On April 5, 1984, Abdul-Jabbar reached back and flipped a modest Skyhook toward the basket from the right baseline. With 8:52 remaining in a game the Lakers would take from the Utah Jazz 129–115 in Las Vegas, the ball dropped through the net and Chamberlain's 31,419-point total was

© Robert Beck/AllSport

Right-handed or left-handed, Kareem Abdul-Jabbar has scored more points than any basketball player in history.

no longer the NBA's highest career scoring total. Chamberlain has always been known as the game's most dominant figure, but, in truth, Abdul-Jabbar needed only one more than Chamberlain's fourteen seasons to surpass the milestone. After the 1987–88 season, the total was 37,634 points. Call Abdul-Jabbar, then, the most consistently excellent offensive player the NBA has ever known.

THE GREATEST
MOMENTS

Certainly, basketball has had its moments over the years. A sampling:

In 1892, basket ball (as it was then known) was unveiled to the public for the first time at the School for Christian Workers in Springfield, Massachusetts. In that initial confrontation, the students beat the teachers 5 goals to 1. Amos Alonzo Stagg, soon to be a famous football coach, prevented an ignominious shutout.

According to archives at the Hall of Fame, the first professional game was played in 1896 at the Masonic Temple Auditorium in Trenton, New Jersey. In 1907, the barnstorming Buffalo Germans began what would grow to a 111-game winning streak. Sixteen years later, the boy's basketball team at Passaic High School in New Jersey

won 159 straight games. In 1927, Abe Saperstein organized the Harlem Globetrotters. Since then, the 'trotters have played to delighted audiences in more than one hundred nations. On December 29, 1934, basketball became a big-time sport. The first college doubleheader, promoted by Ned Irish and played at New York's Madison Square Garden—New York University defeated Notre Dame 25–18, and Westminster edged St. John's 37–33—drew 16,188 fans. The Olympics embraced basketball two years later and the United States won the sport's first gold medal in Berlin. Dr.

James Naismith was on hand to present the medals to the champions. In 1938, Temple University defeated Colorado to win the first National Invitation Tournament at Madison Square Garden. Future Supreme Court justice Byron "Whizzer" White was Colorado's best player. Six-foot-10 George Mikan enrolled at DePaul while 7-foot Bob Kurland joined Oklahoma in 1943, sending basketball into a new era. Two years later, Wyoming University's Kenny Sailors invented the jump shot. In 1946, the Basketball Association of America, the forerunner of today's NBA, was founded, and Hall-of-

Famer Maurice Podoloff was named the first president. The foul lane was widened from six to twelve feet, six years later. In 1953, the Baskin, Louisiana High School girl's basketball team won its 218th straight game. Oscar Robertson, in 1955 became the first college sophomore to lead the country in scoring. He averaged 35.1 points per game for Cincinnati. In 1974, Moses Malone signed with the Utah Stars and became the first professional basketball player to go directly from high school to the pros. In 1982, the University of Kentucky beat Ole Miss 56–49 to become the first college team to record thirteen hundred career victories.

And today, the beat and the bounce go on. What follow are some of basketball's more famous moments.

WILT
CHAMBERLAIN
SCORES 100

MARCH 2, 1962: It happened in Hershey, Pennsylvania on a cold March evening and nobody, including the basketball players gathered there, were particularly happy to be on hand. "There was nothing exciting about the Knicks playing the Warriors in Hershey. Chocolate was more exciting," says York Larese, a role player for Philadelphia. "But the biggest thing in my life was to see *that*."

That was possibly the greatest single-game feat in all of sports history. Never mind that it was a meaningless late-season game that had virtually no effect on the standings. Wilt Chamberlain, the 7-foot-1 center for Philadelphia, scored 100 points that night, an accomplishment that has never been approached. To put that effort in perspective, consider that the second-best total, 73, was achieved twice by Chamberlain and once by David Thompson.

Chamberlain began the game quietly enough, dropping 7 of 14 field goals and uncharacteristically hitting all 9 of his freethrows, for 23 first-quarter points. He added another 18 in the second quarter and recorded 1 of his 2 assists. Chamberlain came out shooting in the third quarter and made 10 of 16 shots. Heading into the final twelve-minute period Chamberlain had 69 points and it was becoming clear that the Warriors had nothing on their mind beyond setting him up. "We'd shoot and Wilt would take off down the court like a lonesome end," says Knicks center Darrall Imhoff. "It was like covering a receiver. It was the hardest I ever saw Wilt work."

The Knicks began holding the ball on offense and fouling Chamberlain's teammates in an effort to hold his scoring total down. Chamberlain, however, kept charging toward

© AP/Wide World Photos

For one game, Wilt Chamberlain played at the level that athletes dream about—he was unstoppable against the Knicks on March 2, 1962.

© AP/Wide World Photos

the basket. "Even when I broke the record I didn't even think of scoring a hundred," Chamberlain said later.

With five minutes left, his count had soared to 89 points. Now Philadelphia Coach Frank McGuire inserted substitutes, instructing them to foul the Knicks, which would stop the clock and hopefully give Chamberlain more opportunities to score. With 2:45 left, Chamberlain hit 90 with a freethrow, then added 2 more foul shots and two fadeaway jumpers to reach 96. With all five Knicks guarding him,

Chamberlain threw down a dunk for 98. With 46 seconds left, backup center Joe Ruklick fed Chamberlain for a power dunk and the unprecedented 100 mark. The game ended right there—Philadelphia 169, New York 147—when many of the 4,124 spectators stormed the court.

"We all knew we were witnessing something extraordinary," Ruklick recalled later. "That game was sort of the apotheosis of what we'd seen all year. We knew this was going to happen."

BOSTON
WINS ITS 8TH STRAIGHT TITLE

Boston Celtics 95, Los Angeles Lakers 93

APRIL 28, 1966: Every sport has its dynasties. Consider the Pittsburgh Steelers of the late 70s, the New York Yankees from 1949–53, or the Montreal Canadiens of 1956–60. Never, however, has a team in major league professional sports dominated its game to the extent the Boston Celtics did from 1958–66. Under Coach Red Auerbach they won eight consecutive NBA championships—a record that may never be equaled, given today's level of competition. How did they do it?

It was the arrival of 6-foot-10 center Bill Russell in 1956 that gave the Celtics a creditable defense to go with scorers Bill Sharman, Bob Cousy, and Tom Heinsohn. Russell provided rebounding and intimidation and Boston won the championship that season, beating St. Louis in seven games. Sam Jones and K.C. Jones arrived over the next two seasons, and Boston continued to win. John Havlicek joined up in the middle of the eight-year reign, bringing new blood to a lineup that was growing old. The infusion worked, and three more titles followed, giving the Celtics a staggering seven straight.

The 1965–66 season was a struggle for the Celtics. Although they went 54–26 that season, they placed a game behind Philadelphia in the Eastern Division. The 45–35 Lakers, meanwhile, coasted to first place in the Western Division with a seven-game lead over Baltimore. The Celtics were lucky to get by Cincinnati in the first round of the playoffs, but Auerbach, down two games to one, elevated Havlicek from his role of sixth man to starter. The change worked magnificently. From that point on, he nearly doubled his rebounding average and led the team in scoring.

© Fred Roe

© Fred Roe

The Celtics won the series 3–2, then dispatched Philadelphia in five games. But when the Lakers won the first two games of the championship series in Los Angeles, the Celtics looked finished. Although they eventually rallied to even the series at three, in the final game their five starters wore eight bandages, Russell was nursing a broken bone

Pensive moments on the bench gave way to a celebration led by center Bill Russell and Red Auerbach (below) after the Celtics won their eighth straight NBA title in 1966.

in this foot, and Sam Jones was starting to look like a weary thirty-two-year-old. Yet, it didn't seem to matter.

The Lakers' brilliant shooters, Elgin Baylor and Jerry West, came out cold, shooting 3 for 18 in the first half. The Celtics built up a big lead and held on for a 95–93 victory. Havlicek and Russell both played the entire forty-eight minutes, and Auerbach could light up his final victory cigar. Under Russell, who would take over as player-coach, the Celtics would win two more titles in three years, giving them eleven championships in Russell's thirteen years—easily the most dominant run in the history of professional sports.

R I C K
BARRY
E N D S
CHAMBERLAIN'S
STRING

ife is full of concessions, and so is professional basketball. Over the 1966–67 season, Wilt Chamberlain sacrificed his whopping scoring average for the collective well-being of the Philadelphia 76ers. It was a reasoned choice, because the 76ers won the NBA championship that year—Chamberlain's first. It also opened the door for a San Francisco forward named Rick Barry, who ended Chamberlain's seven-year grip on the scoring title and with it an entire era.

Chamberlain, the 7-foot-1 center, entered the league in 1959–60 and immediately took control in the scoring column. As a rookie, he averaged 37.6 points a game, 6 more than Cincinnati's runnerup Jack Twyman. A year later, Elgin Baylor would average nearly 35 points a game, but it wasn't enough; Chamberlain managed 38.4. It got worse. Chamberlain's monster season came in 1961–62 when he scored 4,029 points for an average of 50.4. Chicago's Walt Bellamy was a distant second, almost 19 points behind. For another four seasons, Chamberlain pumped out the numbers, averaging 44.8, 36.9, 34.7, and 33.5 points per game. His last scoring title did not come easily; right behind him were Jerry West of Los Angeles (31.3), Cincinnati's Oscar Robertson (31.3), and the NBA's Rookie of the Year, Barry, at 25.7 points per game.

Heading into the 1966–67 season, the 76ers sensed a weakness in the Boston Celtics, who had won eight straight NBA championships. Philadelphia had good scoring depth behind Chamberlain, featuring Hal Greer, Chet Walker, and Billy Cunningham. Through his first seven seasons, Chamberlain averaged 2,438 shots a season and made

approximately 51 percent. This time around, Chamberlain improved his shot selection; he took only 1,150 shots over the course of eighty-one regular-season games and made a searing 68 percent. Chamberlain, who had cleared 4,000 points once and 3,000 twice, totaled 1,956 points for a modest average of 24.1. Thus, the 76ers ran away with the Eastern Division, finishing with a 68–13 record, eight games ahead of the Celtics.

© Manny Rubio

Meanwhile, the Warriors were relying on Barry to carry the scoring load, since center Nate Thurmond was the only other viable producer. When the regular season was over, Barry had blistered the nets at a pace of 35.6 points per game. For the record, even Robertson (30.5) slipped ahead of Chamberlain in the scoring race. Barry's one-man show lifted the Warriors to a 44–37 record and the Western Division title. Fittingly, both Chamberlain and Barry reached the championship series. In the final round, Barry continued to score well, averaging nearly 35 points per game against Philadelphia. But the 76ers, with Chamberlain picking his shots and averaging only 21.7 points an outing, won the series in six games. Barry had ended one of the most dominant scoring runs in sports, but Chamberlain finally had the championship title that meant so much to him.

After seven years with Wilt Chamberlain atop the NBA scoring list, Richard Francis Dennis Barry III broke through with a 35.6-point scoring average in the 1966–67 season.

© Manny Rubio

New York Knicks center Willis Reed inspired teammates with ferocious play (below) against Wilt Chamberlain and the Lakers. Though Reed was called for a loose-ball foul on this play, the Knicks, including teammate Dick Barnett (right) rose to the occasion to win game seven of the 1970 NBA finals.

W I L L I S
REED
I N S P I R E S
T H E   K N I C K S

New York Knicks 113, Los Angeles Lakers 99

© Walter Iooss Jr./Sports Illustrated

MAY 8, 1970: Willis Reed enjoyed the best season of his career in 1969–70, and led the New York Knicks to the NBA championship series with the Los Angeles Lakers. Then, during game six of the series, the 6-foot-10 center turned to drive down the lane for a layup and stretched two muscles in his right thigh in the process. Down he went, writhing in pain. Without Reed to restrain him, Wilt Chamberlain scored 45 points and the Lakers blew out the Knicks 135–113, which set up a final game on May 8 at Madison Square Garden.

With Reed out, the Knicks could be forgiven for thinking all was lost. Yet two hours before the final game, Reed stepped into the quiet arena and, after a brief shooting session, decided he could play. Chamberlain stood watching at the side of the court. "I can't go to my right that well," Reed said as he walked off the court past Chamberlain, drawing a laugh from his rival. That figured, because Reed had never gone to his right particularly well.

Reed informed the Knicks he would play, and the mood in the locker room noticeably brightened. "It's like getting your left arm sewn back on," said Reed's teammate Cazzie Russell. Buoyed, the Knicks ran out to officially warm up, while Reed remained behind and received a pain-killing injection. The Garden crowd, uneasy over Reed's absence, exploded when the big man slowly walked to the Knicks' end of the court with one minute left before tip-off. Even his teammates paused to watch as Reed casually sank his first practice shot. Forward Bill Bradley felt chills as Reed prepared to jump against Chamberlain. "I cannot imagine any place else on earth that I would rather be at this moment than right here," he thought, "about to play in the final game of the championship of the world."

It was Reed who scored the Knicks' first points on a jumper from the top of the key. A minute later, Reed connected on his second and final shot of the game. Soon, he was limping noticeably, then dragging his injured leg up and down the court. Beyond the emotional lift he brought the Knicks, Reed played phenomenally brave defense, limiting Chamberlain to just two baskets in nine shots. When he left the game with 3:05 left in the first half, New York led 61–37, and the team's first championship in twenty-four years of league history was assured.

Guard Walt Frazier scored 23 points in that first half, 13 in the second half, and Dave DeBusschere was also in top form. But, ultimately, it was Reed who made the courageous difference.

THE LAKERS

WIN 33 STRAIGHT

NOVEMBER 5, 1971–JANUARY 7, 1972: Consistency is the most difficult thing to harness in professional sports, but for sixty-four amazing days the 1971–72 Los Angeles Lakers did not lose. Even today their thirty-three-game winning streak stands as one of the great accomplishments in professional athletics.

Los Angeles was 48–34 the year before, so winning wasn't exactly a new phenomenon when they opened the NBA season in 1971. The guards, Jerry West and Gail Goodrich, would supply most of the points, and Wilt Chamberlain would fill the rebounding role. The streak began quietly enough, with a 110–106 victory over Baltimore on November 5. The Lakers found a rhythm, especially on defense, and rolled through the month with fourteen consecutive wins. The offense found itself, too, as evidenced by a 143-point effort against Philadelphia and a 138–121 triumph over Seattle. As the streak grew, so too did the attention on the team. "I played with the Globetrotters when they won 445 in a row," Chamberlain told writers, "and they were all on the road."

But this was for real. On December 10, the Lakers met the Phoenix Suns, winners of eight straight. Digging themselves out of a 14-point hole in the fourth quarter, the Suns forced an overtime period when Los Angeles went the final four minutes and forty-four seconds without a basket. Mel Counts tied the game at 111–all with twenty-one seconds left. Goodrich saved it, though, drilling 3 long jump shots to lift the Lakers 126–117. Two nights later, Atlanta was dispatched 104–95. "This team runs like Boston did a few years ago," said coach Bill Sharman after the twenty-first

© George Long/Sports Illustrated

straight win. "Each man knows what his job is, and he does it, but more than that, we know we can beat anybody."

And the beat went on for another twelve games. The Lakers trashed Philadelphia 154–132 on December 19, and finally, on January 7, handled Atlanta, 134–90, for their thirty-third consecutive victory. In the end, it took a great team, the Milwaukee Bucks, and a great player, Kareem Abdul-Jabbar, to catch up with Los Angeles. Abdul-Jabbar scored 39 points and was the catalyst in an 18–2 fourth-

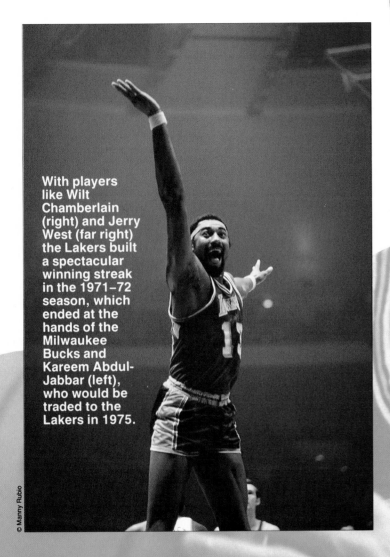

With players like Wilt Chamberlain (right) and Jerry West (far right) the Lakers built a spectacular winning streak in the 1971–72 season, which ended at the hands of the Milwaukee Bucks and Kareem Abdul-Jabbar (left), who would be traded to the Lakers in 1975.

© Manny Rubio

quarter run that put the Lakers away for good. The final score was 120–104.

"We knew the streak had to end some time," Sharman said. "It was one of our weakest games in quite a while, but I think we learned from it. It's hard to learn when you win." And win they did. The Lakers finished the season at 69–13, the NBA's best record ever. Their final victory of the season, over the New York Knicks in the championship series, was almost anticlimactic.

Magic Johnson (below and right) has the size and strength to play center, as he demonstrated against the Philadelphia 76ers in the Lakers' championship series in 1980.

© UPI/Bettmann NewsPhotos

MAGIC
JOHNSON
PLAYS
CENTER

Los Angeles Lakers 123, Philadelphia 76ers 107

MAY 16, 1980: By the time the Los Angeles Lakers had reached the 1980 NBA championship series with the Philadelphia 76ers, they had experienced their share of bad news. Owner Jack Kent Cook had sold the team during the summer. New coach Jack McKinney fell from his bicycle during November and assistant Paul Westhead was forced to take over. And now, before the sixth game of the series, they learned that center Kareem Abdul-Jabbar, their 7-foot-2 tower of strength, would not be able to play as a result of a severely sprained ankle he had incurred during the previous game. The team was understandably upset about the prospect of playing without their star, who had burned Philadelphia for more than 33 points and 13 rebounds over five games.

Enter Earvin "Magic" Johnson. Over the course of the season, Johnson had proved himself to be exceptionally versatile. While Boston's Larry Bird was more visible in winning Rookie of the Year, Johnson averaged 18 points, and approximately 7 rebounds and 7 assists per game. At 6-foot-9, the first pick in the 1979 draft had the body of a forward but the quickness and court vision of a point guard. Could he be a center, too? If anyone could stretch to the role, it would be Magic.

Westhead hoped so, because there was no one on the roster capable of handling the 76ers' massive Darryl Dawkins in the pivot. So Johnson lined up at center and sixth man Michael Cooper, a defensive specialist, started for Johnson at guard. The Lakers led the series three games to two, but this game was at the Spectrum in Philadelphia. With 18,276 mostly hostile fans in the seats, Johnson jumped center opposite Dawkins. His performance, logged over forty-seven of the game's forty-eight minutes, was one for the ages. Carrying the weight of the Lakers' recent playoff miseries—they had won only one league title since the franchise moved from Minneapolis in 1961—Johnson literally did it all.

The astounding numbers: 42 points, on 14-for-23 shooting from the field and a perfect 14-for-14 from the free throw line, 15 rebounds (12 on the defensive end), 7 assists, and 3 steals. Johnson led all players in scoring and rebounding and was chiefly responsible for Dawkins's ineffective 14-point, 4-rebound performance. The Lakers won 123–107, and Johnson was named the series' Most Valuable Player.

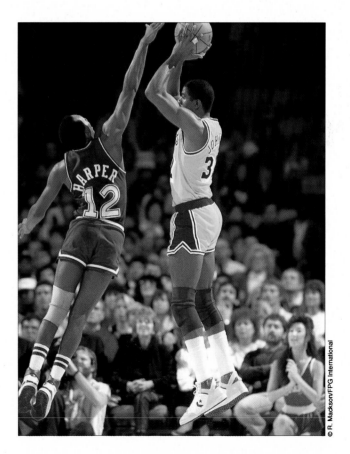

© R. Mackson/FPG International

With the eyes of the world on Barcelona, Michael Jordan was the star that burned brightest on the court for America's Dream Team. Even opponents asked Jordan to pose with them for photographs.

THE
DREAM
TEAM

Any team on which New York Knicks center Patrick Ewing (top left) and Utah forward Karl Malone (bottom left) play is going to have difficulty losing a game.

Tim O'Leff/Sportschrome

When basketball's international governing body voted overwhelmingly to include National Basketball Association players at the 1992 Olympics, suddenly, the rest of the world was playing for the silver medal. This was not an All-Star team, this was a running, jamming, breathing Hall of Fame. Never before had such a roster of basketball talent—or perhaps any athletic talent—been assembled. The names were the Who's Who of basketball: Michael Jordan, Larry Bird, Magic Johnson, Charles Barkley, Patrick Ewing, Clyde Drexler, John Stockton, and more. They were breathtaking to behold. Some opponents, like the Brazilian national team, were so impressed with the United States squad that they requested to have their photos taken with leading lights such as Jordan, Bird, and Johnson.

And when it was over, when the United States dispatched Croatia 117–85 in the gold-medal final, the head coach, Chuck Daly, put America's team in a marvelous perspective. "This was a majestic team," he said. "I understand 180 countries and three billion people watched this game. Somewhere, there's a 12- or 13-year-old kid who dreams of being Magic or Michael or Larry or Patrick Ewing. That's good for the sport. It gives the people a dream, and they're trying to live out a dream."

Dream Team. Perfect. Jordan is likely to go down as the greatest scorer in NBA history, Johnson may well be the game's best guard ever, and Bird could be the most complete player overall. Throw in a David Robinson or a Christian Laettner or a Karl Malone and you have a backup five who could have finished second at Barcelona.

David Leah/Allsport

David Leah/Allsport

Christian Laettner, Duke's marvelous forward, was the token college player on the Dream Team.

The team was assembled amid much speculation and commentary over who should comprise it. Ultimately, it was decided to go with only one collegian, Duke's versatile Laettner. From the beginning, the team dominated the competition and through thirteen games was never seriously threatened. The final against Croatia was a rematch of a blowout earlier in the Olympic tournament. Croatian forward Toni Kukoc, a European star, had been held to a modest four points in the first game. In the final, Kukoc, playing opposite Jordan and Scottie Pippen, started quickly, as did teammate Drazen Petrovic. After ten minutes, Croatia actually led and the billions watching around the world began to wonder if the Dream Team was merely the stuff of imagination.

But late in the first half, the United States put together a 15–2 run and then opened the second half with another 11–2 spurt. The final result, a 32-point victory for the United States, was hardly indicative of the Americans' dominance. Kukoc (16 points) and Petrovic (24 points) were overwhelmed by depth. No fewer than seven Americans scored in double figures: Jordan (22), Barkley (17), Ewing (15), Pippen (12), Johnson (11), Chris Mullin (11), and Drexler (10).

Bird played 12 minutes but did not score in what turned out to be the last game of his career. "If the games were more exciting I think you would have seen a lot more emotion," he said. "When you're winning by 50 every night, it takes something away. The only reason I played was because it was a good way for me to go out this late point in my career. And one thing you can tell your kids is I played on the greatest team of all time."

While Michael Jordan (far left) was the best basketball player at Barcelona, it was the sentimental performances of longtime rivals Larry Bird (top left) and Magic Johnson (bottom left) that made the Dream Team experience special.

AP/Wide World Photos

Wide World Photos

Mike Powell/Allsport

INDEX

Abdul-Jabbar, Kareem, 11, 13–14, *15*, 23, 29, 46, 60, 68, *68–69*, 69, 74–75, *86–87*, 86–87, 89, 92

Adams, Alvan, 70

Ainge, Danny, 17

Alcindor, Lew. *See* Abdul-Jabbar, Kareem

Allen, Forrest C. (Phog), 48

Archibald, Nate, 39

Armstrong, Paul, 65

Auerbach, Arnold Jacob (Red), 11, 16–17, 23, 24, 35, 80–81, *81*

Ausbie, Geese, 56–57

Barker, Cliff, *66–67*

Barnett, Dick, *84–85*

Barry, Rick, 18–19, 82–83

Baylor, Elgin, 18, 20–21, 54, 81, 82

Beard, Ralph, 66, *66–67*, 67

Bee, Clair, 62

Bellamy, Walt, 82

Bianchi, Al, 29

Bird, Larry, 11, 17, 23–24, *25*, 32, 37, 89

Boe, Roy, 32

Bol, Manute, 11

Boston Celtics, 70, 80–81

Bowie, Sam, 39

Bradley, Bill, 26–27, 85

Breuer, Randy, 42

Brian, Frank, 30

Bridgeman, Junior, 14

Brown, Walter, 30

Burke, Glynn, 49

Burns, Gilbert, 43

Chamberlain, Wilt, 11, 18, 23, 24, *26–27*, *28*, 29, 37, 39, 51, 52, 53, 54, 60, 74–75, 78–79, 82–83, 85, 86, *87*

Chaney, Don, 68

Collins, Jocko, 64

Cook, Jack Kent, 89

Cooper, Michael, 89, 92

Costello, Larry, 29

Counts, Mel, 86

Cousy, Bob, 17, 23, 30–31, 46, 51, 52, 80

Cowens, Dave, *70–71*

Cunningham, Billy, 82

Dawkins, Darryl, 89, 91

DeBusschere, Dave, 85

Denver Nuggets, 73

Detroit Pistons, 73, 92

Enberg, Dick, 60

English, Alex, 73

Erving, Julius, 8, 23, 32–33

Fort Wayne Pistons, 64–65

Fouke, Harry, 68

Foust, Larry, 65

Frazier, Walt, 26, 27, 85

Fulk, Joe, 21

Goodrich, Gail, 29, 86

Gottlieb, Leo, 62

Green, Rickey, 60

Greer, Hal, 82

Groza, Alex, 66, *66–67*, 67

Hagan, Cliff, 17

Harlem Globetrotters, 56–57

Harrison, Les, 66, 67

Havlicek, John, 17, 23, 34–35, 70, 80, 81

Hayes, Elvin, 60, 68, *69*, 69

Hayes, Woody, 34

Heinsohn, Tom, 17, 31, 51, 70, 80

Hofheinz, Roy, 68
Holzman, Red, 66
Houston Cougars, 68–69

Imhoff, Darrall, 78
Indianapolis Olympians, 66–67
Irish, Ned, 76

Johnson, Dennis, 17
Johnson, Earvin (Magic), 14, 18, 23, 32, 36, 37,
    46, 88–89, 89–91, 90–91, 92
Jones, K.C., 17, 80
Jones, Sam, 17, 80, 81
Jones, Wah Wah, 66–67
Jordan, Michael, 11, 18, 21, 32, 38, 39

Kauffman, Bob, 41
Kerner, Ben, 44
Kundla, John, 64
Kurland, Bob, 76

Larese, York, 78
Lewis, Guy V., 68–69
Lister, Alton, 42
Long, John, 73

Los Angeles Lakers, 6–7, 80–81, 85, 86–87,
    89–91, 92
Loscutoff, Jim, 17, 51
Loughery, Kevin, 32
Lucas, Jerry, 35

Macauley, Ed, 17
McDaniel, Xavier, 38–39
McDonald, Glenn, 70
McGuire, Al, 69
McGuire, Frank, 79
McHale, Kevin, 17
McKinney, Jack, 89
McMillan, Nathaniel, 38–39
Mahan, Frank, 8
Malone, Moses, 37, 76
Maravich, Pete, 11, 40–41, 46, 47, 56
Martin, Slater, 65, 65
Meminger, Dean, 41
Meyer, Ray, 43
Meyers, Dave, 14
Mikan, George, 42–43, 52, 53, 64–65, 65, 76
Minneapolis Lakers, 64–65
Moe, Doug, 73
Mokeski, Paul, 42

Monroe, Earl, 54–55

Naismith, James, 8, 48, 76
National Basketball Association, 8
New York Knicks, 62–63, 85

Olajuwon, Akeem, 39
Oldham, John, 65

Palmer, Bud, 62
Parish, Robert, 17
Perry, Curtis, 70
Pettit, Bob, 44–45
Philadelphia 76ers, 89–91
Phillip, Andy, 30
Phoenix Suns, 70
Podoloff, Maurice, 76
Powers, Richie, 70, 70–71

Ramsey, Frank, 17, 31
Reed, Willis, 26, 27, 37, 84, 85
Riley, Pat, 32, 92
Risen, Arnie, 66
Robertson, Oscar, 23, 37, 39, 46, 47, 52, 76,
    82, 83

Powers, Richie, 70, *70–71*

Ramsey, Frank, 17, 31
Reed, Willis, 26, 27, 37, *84*, 85
Riley, Pat, 32
Risen, Arnie, 66
Robertson, Oscar, 23, 37, 39, 46, *47*, 52, 76, 82, 83
Robey, Rick, *12–13*
Robinson, David, 91
Rochester Royals, 66–67
Ruklick, Joe, 79
Rupp, Adolph, 48–49
Russell, Bill, 9, 11, 17, 23, 24, 29, 31, 37, 39, 50–51, 74, 80–81, *81*
Russell, Cazzie, 85

Sailors, Kenny, 76
Sampson, Ralph, 42
Saperstein, Abe, 76
Schaus, Fred, 65
Schayes, Dolph, 29, 52–53
Schectman, Ossie, 60, 62
Sharman, Bill, 17, 31, 51, 80, 86, 87
Siegfried, Larry, 35
Silas, Paul, 70
Smith, Dean, 39

Smith, Elmore, 14
Sobers, Ricky, 70
Stagg, Amos Alonzo, 76
Stockton, John, 91
Stutz, Stan, 64

Taylor, Brian, 33
Thomas, Isiah, *72–73*, 73
Thompson, David, 78
Thorn, Rod, 33
Thurmond, Nate, 83
Toronto Huskies, 62–63
Tripucka, Kelly, 73
Twyman, Jack, 29, 82

UCLA Bruins, 68–69

Van Arsdale, Dick, 70
Vandeweghe, Kiki, 73

Walker, Chet, 82
Washington, Miriam, 56
Webb, Anthony Jerome, 8
Wesley, Walt, 14
West, Jerry, 21, 29, 37, 54–55, 74, 81, 82, 86, 87
Westhead, Paul, 89
Westphal, Paul, 70

White, Byron, 76
White, Jo Jo, 70
Wilkens, Lenny, 37
Williams, Pat, 32
Winters, Brian, 14
Woodard, Lynette, 9, 11, 56–57
Wooden, John, 11, 58–59, 68, 69
Worthy, James, *22*

Zaslofsky, Max, 30, 43, 62